# DEMOCRACY

contemp
culture

## BIG IDEAS

*General editor: Lisa Appignanesi*

As the twenty-first century moves through its tumultuous first decade, we need to think about our world afresh. It's time to revisit not only politics, but our passions and preoccupations, and our ways of seeing the world. The Big Ideas series challenges people who think about these subjects to think in public, where soundbites and polemics too often provide sound and fury but little light. These books will stir debate and continue to be important reading for years to come.

Other titles in the series include:

| | |
|---|---|
| Julian Baggini | **Complaint** |
| Jenny Diski | **The Sixties** |
| Ian Hacking | **Identity** |
| Eva Hoffman | **Critical Time** |
| Steven Lukes | **Moral Relativism** |
| Susie Orbach | **Bodies** |
| Slavoj Žižek | **Violence** |
| Renata Salecl | **Tyranny of Choice** |

# DEMOCRACY

Crisis and Renewal

---

Paul Ginsborg

P

PROFILE BOOKS

First published in Great Britain in 2008 by
PROFILE BOOKS LTD
3A Exmouth House
Pine Street
London EC1R 0JH
www.profilebooks.com

1 3 5 7 9 10 8 6 4 2

Typeset in Minion by MacGuru Ltd
info@macguru.org.uk
Printed and bound in Italy by L.E.G.O. S.p.A., Lavis

The moral right of the author has been asserted.

A CIP catalogue record for this book is available from the
British Library.

ISBN 978 1 84668 093 9

The paper this book is printed on is certified by the © 1996 Forest
Stewardship Council A.C. (FSC).
The printer holds FSC chain of custody SGS-COC-2939

FSC
Mixed Sources
Product group from well-managed
forests and other controlled sources
Cert no. SGS-COC-2939
www.fsc.org
© 1996 Forest Stewardship Council

# CONTENTS

To David in his fifteenth year

## PRELUDE: A MEETING OF MINDS

My story begins in London, on a spring evening of 1873. It was a wet but not particularly cold night and the city was enveloped in a humid mist. William Gladstone, the prime minister, was nearing the end of his first and most memorable administration during the long reign of Queen Victoria. In the Commons he had just lost a vote on his Irish University Bill. Further away from the capital, the Ashanti warrior monarch Kofi kari-kari ('King Coffee', as he was called in the British press) was menacing British settlers and interests on the Gold Coast.

Two middle-aged men, one 54 years old, the other 66, meet for the first time. The older man has invited the younger to dinner, at his home in Albert Mansions, Victoria Street. They are both accompanied – the one by his daughter Eleanor, the other by his step-daughter Helen. Of the two men the younger one seems the worse for wear. He is dressed badly, suffers from carbuncles and bronchitis, and has an enormous grey-white beard which is not impeccably clean. He speaks English with a polished German accent; indeed, he is German. The other is extremely English, even if he spends much of the year in the milder climate of Avignon in the south of France, partly for reasons of health and partly to be close to the tomb of his beloved wife, Harriet Taylor, who had died in that city in November 1858. The Englishman is as courteous and correct as the German is impatient and irascible. The one is an intellectual greyhound, the other a bull. They are, with the exception of Charles Darwin, the two greatest minds of the Victorian era.

To begin with, the atmosphere of the meeting is rather embarrassed, even diffident, given the striking contrast in character and beliefs between the two men. Then it warms up, and their mutual curiosity comes to the fore. The older man, who is John Stuart Mill, the foremost liberal thinker of his age (perhaps of any age), had become increasingly interested in socialism, if not in communism. In 1848 he welcomed the revolution in Paris, expressing the hope that the French, in his opinion always in the vanguard of social and political experimentation, would retain the institution of private property, but facilitate 'all possible experiments for dispensing with it by means of association.'[1] Mill was always willing to return to first principles. He remained sceptical of the solutions proposed by 'revolutionary' socialists, as his posthumously published *Chapters on Socialism* was to show.[2] But in July 1870 he had none the less expressed his approval of a document that the General Council of the First International had published on the outbreak of the Franco-Prussian war. It had been written by the second of my protagonists, and no reader will receive a prize for guessing who he is. In his statement on behalf of the First International, Karl Marx stressed the need for the working classes of the two countries, France and Germany, to fraternise instead of to fight. Mill agreed with him.[3]

Both men, albeit in different ambiences and with different intensity, had been active in British politics. Mill had been Liberal Member of Parliament for Westminster between 1865 and 1868. He had presented an important amendment to the 1867 parliamentary Reform Bill, substituting the word 'person' for 'man', with the aim of giving the vote to women on the same bases as those required of male electors. The amendment received the support of seventy-three MPs, including Disraeli. He had also been instrumental in averting clashes between working-class demonstrators and troops after the failure of Gladstone's franchise Reform Bill of 1866. Although sympathetic to the workers' cause, he had persuaded their leaders to abandon ideas for a mass demonstration in Hyde Park: 'No other person, I believe,' he wrote proudly after the event, 'had at that moment the necessary influence for restraining the working-classes, except Mr Gladstone and Mr Bright, neither of whom was available.'[4] As for Marx, he had worked patiently and tenaciously with British artisans and trade unionists to put together the primitive but altogether novel structure of the first working men's International (1864–76).[5]

During their long conversation that evening in March 1873, they touched upon many subjects, and their points of difference and of agreement came to the fore. Marx was not altogether happy with the plain fare that was habitually served at Mill's table. Paul Lafargue, Marx's son-in-law, recounts that Marx had a weakness for 'highly seasoned food such as ham, smoked fish, caviare and pickles. His stomach had to pay forfeit for the colossal activity of his brain.'[6]

It was not easy talking to Marx. In the 1860s Marx's children had played a Victorian parlour game with him called 'Confessions'. They had interrogated him on his preferences. Your favourite colour? 'Red.' Your favourite food? 'Fish.' Your idea of happiness? 'To fight.' Your idea of misery? 'Submission.'[7]

During the meal at Albert Mansions it was Marx who did most of the talking, interspersing his remarks with quotes from his favourite authors – Shakespeare, Dante, Aeschylus, Burns. He was an avid reader of both prose and poetry. Mill listened and smiled gently. Both women, Eleanor Marx and Helen Taylor, said little, though neither was overawed. Marx was fond of saying that 'Children must educate their parents', and he had a tender relationship with all three of his daughters.

Mill tended to put the Taylors – above all the mother but also the daughter – on a pedestal of forbidding dimensions, and simultaneously to abase himself, something Marx would never have dreamed of doing. In his *Autobiography* Mill wrote:

> Surely no one ever before was so fortunate, as, after a such a loss as mine [the death of his wife Harriet], to draw another such prize in the lottery of life – another companion, stimulator, adviser, and instructor of the rarest quality [her daughter Helen]. Whoever, either now or hereafter, may think of me and of the work I have done, must never forget that it is the product not of one intellect and conscience but of three, the least considerable of whom, and above all the least original, is the one whose name is attached to it.[8]

One area of sharp divergence between the two men was economics, but not perhaps in the way we might immediately imagine. Marx was a great believer in the beneficial and progressive power of capitalist production. To understand this it is enough to read the famous passage in the 'Communist Manifesto' where he pays tribute to the extraordinary economic achievements of the bourgeoisie, which in scarcely one hundred years had carried out the 'subjection of nature's forces to man', and 'accomplished wonders far surpassing Egyptian pyramids, Roman aqueducts, and Gothic cathedrals'. For Marx the modern bourgeoisie had created more massive productive forces than had all preceding generations put together.[9] Man was 'Nature's owner', and 'she will behave as he wishes'.[10] Precisely for this reason he believed that a new and culminating phase in world history – that of proletarian revolution – was now on the agenda. The economic and scientific foundations had been laid.

Mill was more cautious and one might say more modern. He tried to explain to Marx that endless growth was a real danger. In the advanced capitalist countries, it was necessary instead to establish a 'stationary state' of the economy, to limit unnecessary growth. Mill enunciated at least three reasons for this: to prevent excessive urbanisation and overcrowding, to stop Nature being used entirely instrumentally, with 'every hedgerow or superfluous tree rooted out', and to avoid the over-valuation of material prosperity.[11]

In 1836, when there was heated discussion of the proposed new railway line to Brighton, Mill found it disgraceful that no one had thought of the need to protect areas of great natural beauty, such as the Vale of Norbury at the foot of Box Hill. As for life in London, he hated what he called the 'trampling, crushing, elbowing and treading on each other's heels' which so characterised modern life.[12] He had an aversion to 'dollar hunters' and in this he was not that far away from Marx.

The two men also, as Paul Smart has pointed out, though coming from quite different traditions – the idealist and the pragmatic – shared an idea of human nature which under-lined human beings' capacity for betterment, and for active, voluntary intervention in the conditions of their existence.[13] Marx, though he had peppered the footnotes of volume I of *Das Kapital* with unflattering comments on Mill's political economy, none the less considered him an opponent to respect. He had noted Mill's insertion of a new section underlining the importance of workers' cooperatives in the 1852 edition of his *Principles of Political Economy*, and in July 1871 Marx told an American journalist: 'He [Mill] has traced one kind of rela-tionship between labour and capital. We hope to show that it is possible to establish another.'[14]

However, it is that part of their discussion concerning democracy which interests me here. I think it would be fair to say, though of course there is much debate on this point, that both men were and weren't democrats. Mill believed in representative democracy and in 1861 had published an extended essay about it, *Considerations on Representative Government*. At the end of its third chapter he had written that 'nothing less can be ultimately desirable, than the admission of all to a share in the sovereign power of the state. But since all cannot, in a community exceeding a single small town, participate personally in any but some very minor portions of the public business, it follows that the ideal type of a perfect government must be representative.'[15] And he wanted, as we have seen, both men and women to vote in that representative democracy.

But – and this is the part where his democratic credentials are found wanting – he also felt passionately that the working classes, men and women, were not yet ready or sufficiently educated for democracy. He was scared of the tyranny of an ill-informed and prejudiced majority and insisted, at least for a period, on an electoral system which weighted votes in unequal fashion: so-called plural voting, which guaranteed greater representation to the cultured classes. Nor was this all. Mill was also convinced that 'the effective direction of public affairs' should be entrusted to a non-elected elite: 'a small number of eminent men; experienced, correctly prepared by their education and their experience, personally responsible to the nation.'[16]

Marx, by contrast, believed in direct or participative democracy, based on the active involvement of all the citizens of a given nation. He thought representative democracy a sham, 'the sophistry of the political state', as he had described it in 'The Jewish Question' (1843); a system in which all men appeared to be politically free and equal, but in which they remained in reality profoundly divided by inequalities of income and differential access to power. Human emancipation could be realised only when this profound separation between political man and man in society, between the abstract '*citoyen*' and the *real* man ('der *wahre* Mensch', as Marx called him), was effectively healed.[17] His insistence on the necessary linking of political and economic democracy is one to which I shall return.

In 1871, two years before Marx and Mill met in London, Marx had perceived in the Paris Commune, the brief and radical insurrection which had engulfed the French capital in the aftermath of the Franco-Prussian war, the embryo of a new, more advanced system of political organisation. The Commune, at long last, as he wrote in his pamphlet 'The Civil War in France', 'supplied the republic with the basis of really democratic institutions'. It was 'the political form at last discovered under which to work out the economical emancipation of labour.'[18] Power was to be de-centralised, a popular militia to take the place of the army, citizens were to participate actively in the decision-making process, delegates (not representatives) were to be paid at only worker's wages, and to be subject to recall by their constituents. Far from participative democracy being possible only in a small city as Mill had maintained, Marx saw the Paris Commune demonstrating its feasibility in a great modern one, and the Paris model being one that could be copied all over a federal France. Economic democracy had not been realised in the Paris Commune, but the political sphere had been brought closer to the needs and the control of the population as a whole.

However, Marx, like Mill, could be said to have a shadow over his democratic credentials, for he had not one but two models of a possible future democracy. His attachment to the idea of the 'dictatorship of the proletariat', a phrase that snaked ominously in and out of his correspondence without ever being systematically developed, promised absolutely no good in democratic terms.[19] Nor is there any evidence in his writings to suggest that his two models – the dictatorship of the proletariat and the Paris Commune – were linked diachronically; proletarian dictatorship was *not* presented by him as the necessary but temporary prelude to popular, decentralised participative democracy. It was simply a different and contrasting model of political organisation, far more centralising, excluding and authoritarian than the Paris Commune. Because Marx never worked systematically on the question of democracy (it was on his highly ambitious schedule for research and writing, but he would probably have had to live to at least a hundred years to have got round to it), it was never very clear which of his two models he preferred, or how, if at all, they were linked.

Neither Marx nor Mill, then, could be called impeccable democrats, at least by the standards of our times, if not theirs. It is worth underlining that the two men shared the same tendency to ascribe to *one class* alone privileged political status and leadership function, only to differ radically as to which class that was – for Mill the enlightened bourgeoisie, for Marx the industrial proletariat. Neither of them was a universalist, in the sense of considering every people and nation equal candidates for democracy. Mill, on the basis of his long experience in the Indian Civil Service, did not hesitate to condemn the excessive power of 'European settlers', who 'think the people of the country mere dirt under their feet', but he had no doubts about the civilising mission of a superior nation, namely Great Britain.[20] And Marx, while exhorting the workers of the whole world to unite, was none the less extremely caustic in his observations about certain nations, Slav ones in particular.

~

That evening in London, after more than one glass of port, Marx attacked Mill on a number of crucial points concerning democracy. He found quite unacceptable Mill's wish to exclude illiterates from the vote, and his insistence on weighting votes unequally. Marx also found it strange that Mill had never paused to contemplate the democratic significance of the Paris Commune of 1871, whereas in 1848 he had welcomed the revolution and the socialist elements within it.

Mill responded with patience and in classic liberal fashion. It was true, he said, that he had not paid enough attention to the Commune. However, he reminded Marx that in October 1872, while still in Avignon, he had replied at length to a letter from Thomas Smith, the secretary of the Nottingham Branch of the International Working Men's Association. Smith had sent him his pamphlet entitled 'Letters on the Commune. The Law of the Revolution; or the Logical Development of Human Society'. Mill wrote back: 'In the principles of the Association I find much that I warmly approve, and little, if anything, from which I positively dissent.' He did, though, object to an overly French use of the concept of Revolution: '"The Revolution" as a name for any set of principles or opinions, is not English.' The French, whom he held in great affection, had been led astray by 'treating abstractions as if they were realities which have a will and exert active power'.[21]

Six months later, at dinner in London, Mill agreed with Marx that the federal system of government which the Communards were suggesting was probably the best way forward. However, he returned to the dangers of the revolutionary process and warned Marx that democracy and proletarian dictatorship had nothing in common. 'The working classes', said

Mill, 'or somebody in their behalf', would create a centralised economy, crush all opposition and demonstrate an 'insensibility towards the suffering of others of which not even Robespierre and Saint-Just were capable'. But then, to sweeten the pill, and bring Marx over to his side, he welcomed what Marx had said to a working-class audience in Amsterdam just six months earlier, on 8 September 1872: 'We do not deny', Marx had proclaimed, 'that there are countries such as America, England and I would add Holland if I knew your institutions better, where the working-people may achieve their goal by peaceful means.'[22] For Mill, that was the sunlit road along which they could walk together.

It was nearly midnight before Karl and Eleanor Marx left Mill's house. Accompanying Marx to the door, Mill quoted a few lines of consolation for them both, ageing intellectuals, still eager to discuss and learn. They were from 'The Two-Part Prelude' of his favourite poet, William Wordsworth:

> Many are the joys of youth, but oh, what happiness to live
> When every hour brings palpable access
> Of knowledge, when all knowledge is delight,
> And sorrow is not there.[23]

Mill was to die just over a month later. He returned with Helen to France, but became ill after a long botanical expedition in the countryside near Orange, undertaken with his friend the entomologist Jean Henri Fabre. Marx, who had neither time nor opportunity nor inclination for botany, was to survive him for another ten years.

∿

The meeting that I have recounted to you never took place. I apologise to experts on Marx and Mill for having taken some liberties and given them some uneasy moments. None the less, every word and position that I have ascribed to the two men reflects accurately their positions. Mill did welcome Marx's statement of 1870 on the Franco-Prussian war; Marx did say in September 1872 that in the advanced capitalist countries the working class could come to power by peaceful means; Mill did write that federalism was the best way forward for France; his favourite poet was William Wordsworth; and so on. The meeting could well have taken place, but it did not. That last March in Mill's home in Albert Mansions had been a busy social time, with regular visitors invited to dinner at seven o'clock. As for Marx, he too became quite sociable in his latter years, even going so far as to accept an invitation to dine at a gentlemen's club from another Liberal Member of Parliament, the very unproletarian Sir Mountstuart Elphinstone Grant-Duff.

I have invented the meeting to introduce the subject of this little book: the nature and possibilities of present-day democracy. Significant issues divided Marx and Mill in 1873 – the extent of the electorate, the political role of different social classes, the nature of economic democracy. But they also had many points in contact – 'the admission of all to a share in the sovereign power of the state', as Mill put it, the need for men and women to be active subjects in both politics and society, the possibility of the working classes exercising political power by peaceful means. None of these objectives has been achieved. Furthermore, over the next hundred years, the two major intellectual traditions of liberalism and Marxism, which were to dominate world politics in the twentieth century, far from converging in any way – as my invented meeting gently suggests they might have done – moved radically apart.

Liberalism and communism could unite their military force to defeat the terrible threat of international Fascism and Nazism, but that was as far as they were able to go.

In 1989 liberal democracy triumphed unqualifiedly over its, by now unpresentable, opponent. But at the moment of its global victory, many of its basic practices have been found wanting, and many of its proudest boasts proved unfounded. Today liberal democracy is highly vulnerable. To protect it adequately, there is urgent need for theoretical discussion and practical innovation. Beginning from Marx and Mill and, to tell the truth, without ever really losing sight of them, this book addresses some of the most pressing questions to have arisen in the history of democracy, and relates them to the possibilities, as well as the dangers, of our own times. It does so with reference to democracy in general, but with a particular eye on European democracies and the destiny of the European Union. And it does so with a particular problem in mind – that of the need to invent new forms and practices which *combine* representative with participative democracy, in order to improve the quality of the first through the contribution of the second.

Democracy has many enemies waiting in the wings: politicians and movements that are for the moment constrained to play by its rules, but whose real animus is quite another – populist, manipulative of the modern media, intolerant and authoritarian. They will seize their chance if we do not reform our democracies swiftly. And nowhere is this reform more needed than in the European Union.

**PART 1**

## THE FIRST PARADOX: DIRECT DEMOCRACY AND COMMUNIST DICTATORSHIP

In the first decades of the twentieth century the idea of democracy as the 'self-government of the producers', which was Marx's description of the Paris Commune, was still much to the forefront, in various guises. We can find it, for instance, in the European factory council movement which enjoyed its decade of glory between 1910 and 1920, that is before, during and immediately after the great cataclysm of the First World War.

However, the fate of democracy in the radical working-class movement was not to be determined in Britain or in Italy, amongst the shipworkers on Clydeside or the metalworkers of Turin, but in the cauldron of the Russian revolution. First in 1905, and then even more so in 1917, soviets, the self-organised democratic councils of workers, peasants and soldiers, had sprung up spontaneously, especially in the major cities.[1] Their political kinship with the Paris Commune was clear for all to see. While Lenin had been suspicious of the soviets in 1905, by the spring of 1917 he was enthusiastic. In April of that year, after he had returned from exile to Russia, he argued that the immediate task facing the Russian proletariat was to bring 'social production and the distribution of products under the control of the Soviets of Workers' Deputies'.[2]

Later in the same year, Lenin published a famous and enigmatic pamphlet, 'The State and Revolution'. Its third chapter is a paean of praise for the various initiatives of the Paris Commune – the democratisation of the army and the judiciary, the election of delegates paid only at workmen's wages, the abolition of high offices of the state etc., all of which aimed at the radical simplification of the functions of the state and the bringing of public administration under the control of ordinary people. 'Democracy', wrote Lenin, 'introduced as fully and as consistently as is at all conceivable, is transformed [in this model] from bourgeois into proletarian democracy; from the state (that is, a special force for the suppression of a particular class) into something which is no longer the state proper.'[3]

Historians have argued long and furiously over the nature and status of this text. Was it merely a piece of propaganda, written by a supremely able and cynical politician, with the aim of winning over to his party's cause the revolutionary masses of Petrograd and Moscow? Was it rather a work of Utopian stamp, of no immediate application? How was it possible that there was no mention at all in the text of the role of the revolutionary party, and this from a leader who had constantly theorised the extraordinary importance of the political party in the revolutionary process? Is this absence explained by mere opportunism or by 'The State and Revolution' being an unfinished work? Is it possible, finally, to take the text at its face value, and accept that at that very particular moment of time, Lenin believed the Paris Commune to be the most attractive and feasible model for post-revolutionary democracy?[4]

I hesitate to offer a categorical answer to these questions. What can be said, though, is that the interpretation which stresses the purely instrumental and opportunist nature of Lenin's text, and of Marx's earlier 'Civil War in France', upon which Lenin based it, seems the least convincing. Lenin certainly did not put democracy at the centre of his political reflection, but both he and Marx, probably in an exaggerated way, believed in the great creative potential of the working classes once they moved into action, in the field of democracy as in others.

In the convulsive months that went from the original February revolution of 1917 through to the early summer of 1918, a system of soviet democracy spread throughout the former Russian empire. It can be considered, for all its limitations, an extraordinarily interesting experiment in participative democracy on the part of a largely illiterate population. As was to be expected, soviets flourished first in the great cities, above all where there was a politically conscious working-class population. In their original form, the soviets were rapid training grounds in democracy. Different parties and viewpoints were represented, and issues were debated and voted upon with notable intensity and passion. Naturally enough, the soviets tended to put local interests in first place, but they also showed themselves capable of running large cities such as Petrograd, and doing so in an entirely innovatory democratic fashion.[5]

The soviets also spread to many parts of the vast Russian countryside. The historian Orlando Figes, no lover of the Bolsheviks, has studied the Volga region during the revolution. He writes: 'The first six months of Soviet rule represent a unique period in the history of the Russian peasantry. During these months, from the establishment of district Soviets in the winter of 1917–18 to the outbreak of the civil war at the beginning of the following summer, the countryside was governed by the peasants themselves.'[6] The peasant soviet assembly usually took place on a Sunday afternoon. Too large to be contained in a single building, it often met in an open field, as its more limited predecessor, the assembly of the peasant commune, or *mir*, had done before it.[7]

This extraordinary wave of participation was to be destroyed by civil war which broke out in the summer of 1918, and by the ever-greater need for central command during it. Precisely these factors, as well as the increasing isolation of the Soviet Union on a world scale, have most often been invoked to explain the shift away from democratic forms to an ever more centralised and authoritarian political system. However, such an explanation for Marxism's democratic default is by no means sufficient, for alongside a material and circumstantial explanation there lies an even more powerful ideological one. The Soviet system of democracy was above all destroyed by the subordinate place that it occupied in the overall political theory of the Bolsheviks. Democracy was never a *sine qua non* of their system, a central pillar of socialist revolution. It was more of an optional extra, the adoption of which could be first suspended in the name of the war, and then endlessly post-poned in the years after 1921.

Behind this profound democratic reluctance there lurked the forbidding presence of Marx's other model – the dicta-torship of the proletariat. Lenin tried to put the two models together: the dictatorship of the proletariat, he argued, *was* the Commune model. But his line of reasoning was not convinc-ing, for it conveniently ignored the ever greater role and power of the Communist Party itself – an organised and authoritar-ian presence which had been completely absent in the experi-ence of the Commune. Writing in the Viennese journal *Neue Zeit* in 1904, the German socialist Rosa Luxemburg had fore-seen with extraordinary acumen where all this was leading: from the dictatorship of the party, which would take the place of the proletariat, to the dictatorship of the central commit-tee, which would take the place of the party.[8] And thirty years earlier John Stuart Mill, as we have seen, already had his liber-tarian antennae finally attuned to the probable consequences of a central government, acting in the name of the working-class, which took possession of all the property of the country and administered it for the general benefit. 'Those who would play this game', he wrote mildly but firmly, 'must have a serene confidence in their own wisdom on the one hand and a recklessness of other people's sufferings on the other.'[9]

~

Before leaving the Russian and the Marxist tradition, it is worth commenting a little more upon the system of Soviet democracy as it was enshrined in the constitution of July, 1918. The new constitution, as so often happens, was far removed from historical reality, for it made no mention of the role of the increasingly dictatorial Communist Party. None the less, it represents an important formal attempt to link organs of popular participation to the new institutions of the state. The soviets were recognised as organs of self-government at a local level, institutions of the state which insured that all the working population was to be involved in the process of government.

In the realm of democratic theory the constitution had a number of flaws which are worth reflecting upon. In the first place, it was based upon an institutional pyramid, with the mass of the electors usually exercising their voting rights only at the first, local level. Elections to the All Russian Congress of Soviets were meant to be direct, but very often delegates were chosen by the provincial and urban soviets. This indirect, pyramid system of representation had already been widely criticised in nineteenth-century European constitutional thought.[10]

The Soviet system also adopted a weighting of votes which was utterly incompatible with the basic democratic principle of one person, one vote. Elections for the All Russian Congress of Soviets were organised on the basis of one delegate for every 25,000 inhabitants of urban centres, but only one for every 125,000 peasants.[11] Such a system had obviously been devised to ensure that the core proletarian vote was not swept away by the more conservative peasant one, but it was not a system that could easily claim superiority to Western parliamentary representative democracy. Furthermore, class enemies were to be excluded from the vote, though it was far from clear who was to identify these 'exploiters of the toiling masses', and on what bases. Thus in three crucial areas of democratic theory, the Soviet system came up on the wrong side: on direct and indirect elections, the weighting of the vote, and the exclusion or inclusion of different sections of the population.

I have paused to consider the solution adopted by Lenin and the Russian communists to the question of democracy because of its enormous significance on a world scale. His solution was the one to be adopted, naturally with country-specific variations, in the whole of the communist world between 1921 and 1989: authoritarian single-party states ruled by privileged party oligarchs in the name of the toiling masses – the exact opposite of the Paris Commune.

At the Ninth Congress of the Italian Communist Party in 1960, its leader, Palmiro Togliatti, presented in optimistic and painstakingly statistical terms the long forward march of 'socialism' in world history. By that year, according to Togliatti's calculations, capitalist countries covered 53.5 million square kilometres of the earth's surface, compared to the socialists' 35.2 million; but in terms of population the socialist countries could count on 989 million human beings, while the capitalist ones contained only 824.5 million. In the Soviet Union, insisted Togliatti, the communist regime 'has led not only to the disappearance of the misery and indigence of the working population, but also of all ignorance, illiteracy and cultural backwardness'.[12] It was a pity, though, that he did not pause to discuss what sort of political regimes constituted this triumphant modern-day socialism, and what elements of democracy, if any, were present in them. An honest reply could only have been highly embarrassing.

In March 1989 Mikhail Gorbachev organised, for the first time in seventy years, the first properly democratic elections in the Soviet Union. By then it was too late, and the regime disintegrated in the face of the multiple requests for liberty of every sort. In China the Communist Party leadership took no such risks, closing its ranks in face of the students' requests for democracy, and eventually massacring a significant number of them in Tienanmen Square on 4 June 1989. Almost twenty years earlier, in March 1971, the Chinese had successfully launched their second space satellite. That year was the centenary of the Paris Commune, and to mark the occasion one of the flags from the Commune had been reverentially enclosed in the capsule of the satellite.[13] No symbolic gesture could have been more inappropriate. China has rapidly developed into one of the great economic forces of the world, but in political terms it has remained very much the daughter of twentieth-century communism.

## 2

## THE SECOND PARADOX: THE SIMULTANEOUS
## TRIUMPH AND CRISIS OF LIBERAL DEMOCRACY

The liberal tradition, too, soon established its own ortho-
doxies, foreclosing on the socialist sympathies and many of
the more progressive elements of Mill's political thought.
Liberalism moved, very slowly and with considerable difficulty, towards representative democracy based on universal
suffrage. In many countries, and for many decades, it too
imposed its categories of exclusion from the right to vote.
These were, broadly speaking, fivefold in kind: insufficient
economic capital, measured in terms of property or income
qualifications; lack of cultural capital – with literacy being the
key discriminating factor; belonging to the 'wrong' sex, an
exclusion which had widely differing application, with New
Zealand enfranchising women as early as 1893, but Switzerland only managing to do so in 1971; ethnicity, where the
racist exclusion of poor and downtrodden ethnic minorities
was generally and vigorously applied, as in the United States
for much of its history; and, finally, political opinion, a category of exclusion which was to be widely employed in the
twentieth century, principally against communist and fascist
parties of one sort or another.[14]

In spite of these multiple and often overlapping exclusions,
the forward march of representative democracy, which was
always the preferred democratic form of the liberal camp, was
unmistakable. Representative democracy may be usefully and
immediately defined here as denoting a system which satisfies
the following criteria: a representative government chosen by

an electorate consisting of the entire adult population, whose votes carry equal weight and are cast by secret ballot at regular intervals, and who are allowed to vote for any opinion without intimidation either by the state itself or by organised elements of society.[15] This definition concentrates above all on the minimum requisites of the electoral process of representative democracy. It should be considered as a starting point for our discussion of the possibilities of modern democracy, not as encapsulating its essence once and for all.

This sort of democracy, or rather approximations to it (for our definition is more rigorous than it at first appears, and Mill's own version would not qualify), spread slowly around the world. By 1926 there were twenty-nine countries which boasted broadly convincing democratic credentials. By 1942, at the height of the Second World War, that number had shrunk to just twelve. The democracies survived that darkest hour, and once Hitler had been defeated they enjoyed a new period of expansion, though obviously not in the communist bloc. By 1988, sixty-six out of the then total of 167 members of the United Nations could broadly be considered representative democracies.[16]

This was distinct progress, but it should be noted that in such democracies, the space allowed either in theory or in practice for direct participation in government was minimal. Democracy was representative democracy, tout court. Government and decision-making were the responsibility of representatives, and the task of citizens was to vote occasionally though regularly to choose those representatives.

To bring out the importance of this narrowing down of democracy's scope, I must pause for a moment and look backwards to an older debate and a famous distinction: that between the 'liberty of the ancients' and the 'liberty of the moderns'.

---

Benjamin Constant, addressing the Athénée Royale in Paris in 1819, had made the distinction with crystalline clarity, and his words have echoed down to us for nearly two centuries. In small communities, argued Constant, direct democracy on the Athenian model was possible, but in large-scale and complex modern societies only representative government, *on behalf of* rather than *by* citizens, was feasible. No longer obliged to participate in government, men would be allowed, in Constant's words, 'the enjoyment of security in private pleasures'.[17] But in this way, politics and everyday life, the taking of decisions in the public sphere and the ordinary daily activities of individuals and families were formally separated.

Constant, to do him credit, saw the pitfalls. At the end of his speech of 1819 he urged citizens to exercise an 'active and constant surveillance' over their representatives and warned, in prophetic tones: 'The danger of modern liberty is that, absorbed in the enjoyment of our private independence, and in the pursuit of our particular interests, we should surrender our right to share in political power too easily'.[18] And Mill, who loved Athens and its form of democracy, but thought it impracticable in complex modern societies, none the less urged the citizens who enjoyed modern liberty to take part in public deliberations and democratic duties.

~

Liberal political thought slowly assumed its distinctive form. The public and the private sphere were clearly separated, with women very substantially confined to the second. Citizens were in general to be guaranteed extensive civil rights and privacy by the liberal state, but they were not to play an active part within it. Instead, those who had the right to vote were to elect their representatives to Parliament, but these representatives, called upon to decide on complex national matters, had necessarily to enjoy considerable autonomy of action and opinion from those who had elected them. Lastly, citizens were asked, though not by all liberal theorists, to be vigilant and active in public matters, though the exact form of their involvement was most often left unspecified.

Let me return to my narrative. By the second half of the twentieth century liberalism, like Marxism, had established its own orthodoxy, but there can be little doubting which was the superior model in democratic terms. The Marxist trajectory had been the story of a tragic and irredeemable decline, from the initial welcoming of the Paris Commune and the early soviets to the establishment of communist dictatorship. By the end of the twentieth century communist regimes everywhere were characterised by grey conformity and brutal repression, and in Berlin by a wall which witnessed the deaths of many young people on and around it while they tried to escape to freedom.

The trajectory of liberal democracy, on the other hand, had been unmistakably if not always impeccably upwards, towards the overcoming of those exclusions which I mentioned above, and which had marked and marred so much of its history. During and above all after the Second World War significant further progress took place. Not only did liberal democracy come to guarantee greater civil and political rights to both women and men than any other political system, but it also moved firmly onto the terrain of social citizenship and the welfare state. Emblematic of this shift was William Beveridge's famous report on Social Insurance and Allied Services, first published in the bleak year of 1942. A democracy newly sensitive to social needs was to sweep away the five giants that stood in the way of reconstruction – want, ignorance, squalor, idleness and disease. 'A revolutionary moment in the world's history', proclaimed Beveridge, 'is a time for revolutions, not for patching.'[19] In the Communist regimes of eastern Europe, it is true, citizens also enjoyed some social rights, but they completely lacked both civil and political ones. If one is writing a comparative history of democracy, then the events of 1989–91 and the demise of Soviet and east-European Communism can come as no surprise at all.

~

However, with one of those strange and unexpected twists of history, what followed was not simply the victory of one global political regime over another. Rather, in the decade after the fall of the Berlin Wall, liberal democracy itself entered into profound crisis. This was not a crisis of *quantity*; quite the opposite. In the twelve years after the dismantling of the Wall, representative democracy expanded exponentially, until by the year 2000 120 out of the 192 nation-states of the United Nations could broadly be defined as democratic. For the first time democracy had acquired majority status on a world scale.[20]

The crisis, rather, was one of *quality*. While formal, electoral democracy expanded with great rapidity all over the world, disaffection grew in democracy's traditional heartlands. It was expressed in a number of different ways – declining voter turnout, declining membership of parties, loss of faith in democratic institutions and in the political class in general. Let me take just one example, from one of the most robust of Europe's democracies – Sweden. In 1968, 60 per cent of the respondents to the Swedish Election Study said that political parties were interested in people's opinions, not just their votes. By 1994 that percentage had declined dramatically to 25. A similar decline was to be found in regard to the activities of the Riksdag, the Swedish parliament.[21]

The reasons for such discontent are many, and they have been the subject of much recent scientific attention. Here I wish to concentrate on a number of structural causes. The first was always implicit in representative democracy, but has now assumed an almost universal character: the assignation of politics to a separate sphere, inhabited by professionals, organised by party elites, protected by the technical language and bureaucratic practice of administrators, and to a very great extent impermeable to the general public. Political parties, once mass organisations representing differing voices and interests in society, have retreated increasingly into the institutional sphere, to emerge only at election time. Simultaneously, citizens have withdrawn into the private sphere. The result is that modern democracy has been 'hollowed out'.[22] Back in 1861 Mill was convinced that the essence of liberal democracy in its representative form was quite otherwise:

> The meaning of representative government is, that the whole people, or some numerous portion of them, exercise through deputies periodically elected by themselves, the ultimate controlling power, which, in every constitution, must reside somewhere. This power they must possess in all its completeness. *They must be masters, whenever they please, of all the operations of government.*[23]

Few and foolhardy persons would be prepared to maintain that nowadays democracy, anywhere, corresponds to Mill's meaning.

Secondly, the structural confinement of politics to a privileged and remote sphere has been reinforced by rapid changes in cultural and social habits. Consumer capitalism has had major effects upon the nature of our democracies: the accentuation of home living, of patterns of 'work and spend', which make our societies rich in comforts but poor in time, of individual and family self-celebration and self-interest, of increased television viewing and dependence, have all combined to produce an extraordinary passivity and disinterest in politics. Sometimes modern electorates are capable of mass mobilisation – the US presidential election contest between George W. Bush and John Kerry in 2004 and the battle at the 2008 Democratic primaries between Hillary Clinton and Barack Obama were both bitterly contested – but the general patterns are otherwise.

A special role in this process has been played by television, and by commercial television in particular. Its iron logic dictates that programming is always dependent upon maximising the size of an audience, so that viewers are considered primarily as market members, not citizens. This fundamental choice then determines all the rest: advertisements advocating consumption invade every moment of screen time, and programmes are primarily planned as entertainment and distraction, not information or instruction, especially at peak viewing times. Public television corporations in different nations for a time resisted this logic and practice, but they too have succumbed to a greater or lesser extent. A very strong cultural model on a global level has been established, and there is little space for democratic politics in it. Where politics does survive, it has become media and personality politics, to be viewed rather than experienced.

Furthermore, those oligarchs who control modern television have their own political agendas, which have little to do with liberal democracy as Mill construed it. The role of reasonably autonomous public broadcasting – never a universal feature of modern democracies – diminishes daily. Discussions of its privatisation are frequent, as are the controls exercised upon it. Sometimes a television tycoon uses his personal fortune to invade the sphere of democratic politics and public broadcasting; sometimes the reverse happens, with an over-powerful politician bringing independent broadcasting and journalism to heel. Not by chance are Vladimir Putin and Silvio Berlusconi good friends.

The mention of these two oligarchs brings me to a third structural cause of democracy's crisis (the first two being the confining of politics to a separate sphere, and the rapid growth of consumerism and home living). Politics and plutocracy have joined hands, with the outcome of elections ever more dependent upon big, or very big money. Marx's comments on 'the sophistry of the political state', briefly mentioned above, have much to commend them some 170 years later. Individuals are formally equal at the moment of voting. They each, to put it in Marx's terms, put on their 'lion's skin' for election day; they appear at that moment to be 'truly sovereign', as Mill fondly imagined them. But they are and remain utterly unequal in society, with quite different capacities to influence, or direct, or be a protagonist of the electoral process. Modern elections are not fought on level playing fields, and electoral spending in nearly all democracies has spiralled completely out of control.

In the presence of enormous private funding, democracy and cronydom have come to intertwine. You win elections in order to govern, but also to award lucrative contracts to those who have financed you, or else to place your friends, and in many democracies your relatives, in positions of power and prestige.

Once upon a time mass parties with very large member-
ships exercised some form of control over these processes.
Not that they were democratic. The great German sociologist
Robert Michels, analysing at the beginning of the last century
the German Social Democratic party (the SPD), taught us just
how difficult it is, even for parties with socialist aspirations, to
be democratic.[24] But at least mass 'democratic' parties in some
way represented in the political arena the needs and desires of
their members. Today the parties, much reduced in membership, are further away from society and much more the privileged distributors of the resources of the state. The slippery
slope of corruption beckons to all. In the face of these developments, the ordinary citizen castigates the political class,
but secretly (or openly) desires to climb on, or at least hang
on, to one of the many clientelist ladders which constitute the
hidden, inner mechanisms of very many 'democratic' states.

A final fundamental weakness lies with the changed historical role of the most powerful and, in a former era, most
vibrant democracy in the world – that of the United States. In
1942 the USA's entry into the Second World War under Fran-
klin D. Roosevelt was seen as an imperative for the future of
humanity and her soldiers were greeted as liberators across the
whole of the European continent. Nowadays a considerable
segment of world public opinion views and judges the actions
of the United States in a very different way. It remonstrates with
the USA for having waged, in the name of democracy, disas-
trous and unjustified recent wars, principally in Vietnam and
Iraq. National and imperialist interests have been passed off
as universal, democratic ones. Furthermore, the United States
has boycotted, on the grounds of non-interference in its own
internal affairs, some of the most important initiatives which
have moved in the direction of global governance – the Kyoto

Agreement, the International Criminal Court, the democratic reform of the United Nations. Apart from Somalia, the USA is the only nation not to have ratified the UN Convention on the Rights of the Child. Such refusals have managed to cast doubts even on the *reasonableness* of democratic states. As John Dunn has written, we have chosen 'out of the entire prior history of human speech, this single, for so long so baleful, Greek noun [democracy], to carry this huge weight of political hope and commitment'.[25] The misdirected world role of the USA has done much to undermine that hope.

# 3

## THE DEMOCRATIC DEFICIT OF THE EUROPEAN UNION

Finally, in this catalogue of woes, it is necessary to consider briefly another giant on the world stage, but a sleeping one with regard to the questions being aired here. The European Union is in many ways an extraordinary achievement. Ancient, proud and aggressive nation-states have been led, not by the force of arms, but rather by the gentler methods of persuasion and consent, to pool their resources, work together and surrender at least part of their respective sovereignties. A growing literature sings the praises of Europe's achievement. Europe is 'transnational', 'orchestral', 'networking'; it is based on a high level of social solidarity; it is to be compared favourably with the imperial and aggressive United States, and the repressive and monolithic China. Of the three great world forces which will dominate the twenty-first century Europe, it is often said, is by far the best.[26]

However, the sort of democracy that the European Union practises is limited, indirect and highly unsatisfactory. To understand why this is so, we must return briefly to its origins. The European communities which came into being in 1957 – the EEC (European Economic Community) and Euratom (European Atomic Energy Community) – had, as their names suggest, strictly economic objectives. Right from the start, the European project, and the language it adopted, separated out the needs of political economy from those of liberal democracy. Decisions were taken by administrative and governmental elites, without any desire to make them the result of due democratic process or of public political debate. In this scheme of things, the administrative elite of the European Commission was granted great powers, while the European Parliament was originally assigned only a limited and consultative role. Direct elections to it were held only from 1979 onwards. In the trade-off between economic dynamism and democracy, a dilemma to which I shall return, the founders of Europe clearly chose the first.

This initial democratic deficit was to weigh heavily on the ensuing history of the Union. The separateness of the decision-making sphere, already pronounced in national representative democracies, became macroscopic in the case of European institutions. The Council of the European Union, its most powerful body, composed of ministers from each member country, has been described as being more of a cabal than a cabinet, more of a permanent diplomatic conference than a senate. It is directly accountable to no one and yet legislates profusely.[27] Its guiding principle, intergovernmentalism, that is exclusive collective decision-taking by governing elites, does not lie easily with parliamentary democracy.

Overall, the relationship between the three principal decision-making bodies of the Union – the Council, the Commission and the Parliament – is a complex and uneasy one, with Parliament still the junior partner. The proliferation of a whole range of so-called 'non-majoritarian institutions', such as the European Central Bank or Europol, as well as the many new regulatory agencies, means that key decisions are consistently taken by non-accountable bodies. At the centre of legislative power lie the Committees of Permanent Representatives (COREPER), key enclaves in which the functionaries of the Commission meet and do battle behind closed doors with the emissaries of the Council.[28] Political scientist Peter Mair is right when he stresses in a recent article that the EU's overall structure not only does not take on board participatory democracy, but has grave difficulties even with according space to representative government.[29]

The European elections of 2004 saw appallingly low turnout, even in the European Union heartlands: Holland, Portugal, Sweden, Great Britain dipped under 40 per cent, Germany, Austria, Spain, Denmark and France under 50 per cent. The decline in voter turnout since the first European elections of 1979 has been very marked. The situation was worse still among the new entrants from eastern Europe: only 38.5 per cent voted in Hungary, 28.3 in the Czech Republic, 20.9 in Poland, 17 in Slovakia. Although there are many reasons for these figures, there is one that all shared – the feeling among large swathes of the European electorate that participation in the democratic process had little meaning. The existing gap between the citizens of Europe and their institutions is too great, and this alienation was dramatically revealed when the French and Dutch electorates voted against the proposed European Constitution in referenda in May and June of 2005.[30]

After they had recovered from the shock, the EU elites decided to abandon the ill-fated Constitution, but instead to encapsulate its main provisions in a treaty, one of the many which have marked the history of the Union from its inception. On 13 December 2007 the leaders of the twenty-seven member states signed the Treaty of Lisbon. Only the British prime minister, Gordon Brown, arrived late, revealing yet again that extraordinary mixture of arrogance and diffidence which has characterised British attitudes to Europe. Brown eventually signed the Lisbon Treaty in a restaurant. The Treaty will not come into force until and unless it is ratified by each of the EU's member states. It is up to each country to choose the procedure for ratification, but more than one political leader in Europe, Brown included, is now convinced that it is much better *not* to ask the opinion of national electorates about major European constitutional arrangements.

Over the years piecemeal attempts have been made to reduce the 'democratic deficit'. The European Parliament has seen its powers gradually increase, and the Amsterdam Treaty of 1997 made a strong commitment to greater transparency in decision-making. The Lisbon Treaty will incorporate the Charter of Fundamental Rights into EU law. Yet the single most serious, or at least most publicised, attempt to meet the specific problems posed here – the introduction of the principle of subsidiarity – has been a resounding failure.

Subsidiarity, much stressed in the Maastricht Treaty of 1993, has been obscure in meaning and vague in application. The word itself derives from the Latin *subsidium*, which in military terms signified reserve troops, and the word subsidiary generally evokes the idea of an auxiliary or subordinate function. However, this is not the meaning in EU jargon. Rather, it is meant to convey the principle of delegating to lower bodies in a decision-making pyramid any decision that need not be taken by higher ones. In this sense 'subsidiarity' is derived from its use in Catholic canon law, a legal tradition which boasts no great democratic pedigree, and its most cited historical usage is that of Pius XI in his Encyclical *Quadragesimo Anno* of 1931. Pius, anxious to find a *modus vivendi* with Fascism while protecting the freedom of action of Catholic associationism and family life, asserted that it was wrong to ascribe 'to a greater or higher society', the state, that which 'minor or lower communities' could do by themselves.[31]

This is the principle of subsidiarity, but its application to European democratic practice has, not surprisingly, proved less than satisfactory. Antonio Estella, in his recent study of the use of subsidiarity in the rulings of the European Court of Justice, has concluded laconically: 'Functionally speaking, the principle seems devoid of any clear legal content, which makes its implementation problematic.'[32] And the liberal scholar Larry Siedentop, in his splendid diatribe *Democracy in Europe*, has noted caustically that subsidiarity does not appear to have prevented the Catholic Church from being one of the most centralised – and we must add gerontocratic and gender-biased – decision-making bodies in the world.[33]

Democracy, representative or participatory, is thus little present in the structure of the European Union. Furthermore, the social rights which were so much part of modern European democracy after the Second World War, which so permeated Beveridge's famous report on Insurance and Allied Services and which lay at the heart of the 'social Europe' of both Jean Monnet and Jacques Delors, have come under increasing attack over the last twenty years. Prevailing economic ortho-doxy has condemned the whole idea of the public provision of services. By the 1990s the European Commission was openly committed to privatisations on principle. As Perry Anderson has written, 'The very term "reform" now means, virtually always, the opposite of what it denoted fifty years earlier: not the creation but the contraction of welfare arrangements once prized by their recipients.'[34] European welfare democracy, still presented as the major hallmark of the continent's superiority, is being eroded from within. Only stubborn resistance from local populations, as well as professionals and workers in the public sector, have prevented worse damage being done.

Recently, the eminent banker Tommaso Padoa-Schioppa, who represented Italy on the board of the European Bank from its inception, has diagnosed the European Union as suffering from an acute bout of melancholy. All the primary symptoms are there: loss of faith, inertia, lack of interest in the outside world, introspection and low self-esteem. 'It is not the limited dimensions of the work already undertaken which *justifies* melancholy,' argues Padoa-Schioppa, 'but rather melancholy which stops us from completing the task.'[35] Melancholics, if Plato is to be believed, are capable of sudden and furious bouts of action and spiritual exaltation which enable them to break out of their torpor and move on. Padoa-Schioppa wants to see something like this happening in Europe now. It is difficult to disagree with him, but on the specific question of democracy we must first of all realise that Europe has been built on sand. It is possible to move forward in this field only by radically rethinking the ways in which European citizens can, for the first time, effectively be linked to their political institutions. Without that rethinking, disaffection and torpor can only continue. 'Let us go back to first principles,' as John Stuart Mill would have said.

**PART 2**

# 1

## DEMOCRACY AT THE CROSSROADS

What, then, is to be done? The difficulties facing modern democracy, not just in Europe, are not contingent or mechanical ones, nor a question of mere institutional engineering. They are of a deeper nature. My starting point in tackling them relates back to one of those key factors in democracy's crisis which I outlined in this book's first section – the widespread passivity and indifference to politics prevalent among the majority of the population in democratic countries.

In analysing the causes of this disaffection and what we can do about it, it is necessary to say something, however briefly, about global trends in the last twenty-five years. They do not all point in the same direction, but overall they cannot be said to have helped to make democracy more vital or more present in people's lives. Capital's increasing concentration on a world scale, the result of continuous fusions and takeovers, a process which Marx foresaw with great clarity, has produced new and extraordinarily powerful economic oligarchies. Transnational companies are not the only economic form of organisation present in the current phase of capitalism, but in symbolic terms they are its best representative. In 2001 fifty-one of the hundred biggest economies in the world were transnational corporations, while only forty-nine were national states, and the hundred largest corporations now control about 20 per cent of global foreign assets.[1] They are juggernauts in economic performance but dinosaurs in terms of democracy.

Unstable beasts, they stalk the globe in search of new markets and profits. Theirs is a great unaccountable power. They are able to shift vast resources, decide the fate of entire communities, and dictate their own 'flexible' rules in many parts of the world. In their shadow, the individual citizen feels powerless and dependent at the same time. Neo-liberal economics has fattened these creatures up on a global diet of deregulation. J. S. Mill would have been horrified that the very word 'liberalism', even with a 'neo-' preceding it, could be employed in such a context.

At the same time, the extraordinary growth of consumer capitalism has served in the developed countries as a great compensatory factor for the feeling of powerlessness and precariousness which neo-liberalism has done so much to create. As I mentioned earlier, families and individuals have sought comfort, protection, distraction and entertainment in the joys of home living, and in the purchase of the commodities of every sort which go to create it. There is nothing intrinsically wrong in this at all. Indeed, if one thinks of the great material deprivations of most of the European population less than a hundred years ago, then today's prosperity is cause for great celebration. What is deeply worrying, though, is that there are all too few public spheres in daily life, in the sense of spaces and processes of discussion, democratic debate, and participation. Citizens are overwhelmingly privatised in their habits, thoughts and daily practices.

It is certainly true that levels of education are rising all over the world, and that the internet and many other instruments are democratising access to information, but the largest single cultural influence on families, and in a majority of cases the only cultural instrument in their homes, remains the television. Given the oligarchic structure and conformist culture of global television – Rupert Murdoch's media empire is the classic example of the enormously powerful transnational media company – there is little to hope for from these quarters in terms of a solid transmission of plural, democratic and participative values. Usually, quite the opposite is the case.[2]

So great are these countervailing forces to democratic practices that the strong temptation exists for the average citizen, even if educated and aware, to renounce any time-consuming commitment to activities which extend beyond the narrow circles of home, work, family and friends. 'What difference can I make?' is a frequent and plaintive cry. However, battles against seemingly impossible odds are an obstinately recurring feature of human history, and there are good reasons why the story of David and Goliath has enjoyed such enduring popularity. Where now are our democratic Davids, and how best can they be drawn into a campaign to protect and develop democracy?

## ACTIVE AND DISSENTING CITIZENS

It is not Marx but Mill, with his fierce concentration on the potential of individuals, who gives us the first indications of the road we must travel. It is he who has the clearest idea of what sort of individuals democracy needs, and what sort it could in turn foster. He wrote of the need for citizens to be self-dependent, 'relying on what they themselves can do, either separately or in concert, rather than on what others can do for them'.[3] It was no good, said Mill, for citizens to be like 'a flock of sheep innocently nibbling the grass side by side'.[4] Instead they had to be active and critical, organising and educating themselves – being in substance self-disciplined and self-dependent. Mill wanted no one to conform to custom *as* custom. He loved eccentrics rather than conformists; he wanted everyone to make up their minds on the basis of information and deliberation. He abhorred the type of person 'who lets the world or his own portion of it, choose his plan of life for him . . . [who] has no need of any other faculty than the ape-like one of imitation'.[5] At the end of the famous third chapter of *On Liberty*, entitled 'Of individuality, as one of the elements of well-being', he wrote:

> If resistance waits till life is reduced *nearly* to one uniform type, all deviations will come to be considered impious, immoral, even monstrous and contrary to nature. Mankind speedily becomes unable to conceive diversity, when they have been for some time unaccustomed to see it.[6]

The relevance of these reflections for our society based, as it is, on the conformities of mass consumption and on great passivity in the public sphere hardly needs pointing out.

Mill's identification of the cultural formation and general outlook of active and dissenting individuals is very valuable. It enables us to form an idea of what democratic citizenship *could* be, but by and large is not. Humility, imagination and scepticism are the virtues that Mill requests from citizens.[7] And in one of his most radical works, *The Subjection of Women* (1869), he also gives us a wonderful political glimpse of what he calls 'the true virtue of human beings':

> But the true virtue of human beings is fitness to live together as equals; claiming nothing for themselves but what they as freely concede to every one else; regarding command of any kind as an exceptional necessity, and in all cases a temporary one; and preferring, whenever possible, the society of those with whom leading and following can be alternate and reciprocal.[8]

Sadly, though, he concludes that 'To these virtues, nothing in life as at present constituted gives cultivation by exercise'.[9] And if that was true in an age of liberalism, how much truer still is it in an age of neo-liberalism!

Our problem, then, is brilliantly outlined by Mill. He gives *identity* to the subjects of democratic transformation – active and dissenting individuals – and *content* to the virtues on the basis of which the public, democratic sphere could and should be reorganised. But the key connecting passages – how to create such citizens, and how to bring into being a public democratic sphere of this sort – are, as we shall see, left largely unresolved.

# 3

## FROM ATOMISED FAMILIES TO A
## 'SYSTEM OF CONNECTIONS'

It is to Mill's great credit that at the end of the same passage in *The Subjection of Women* he recognises the family as a key institution in any process of political transformation. Very often in history, he says, the family has been a school of despotism, in which the 'virtues of despotism, but also its vices' have been amply practised. But the family need not necessarily be despotic; rather if it was 'justly constituted', it could be 'the real school of the virtues of freedom'.[10]

Unfortunately, this was an insight which was left undeveloped in Mill's work. Our other Victorian authority, Karl Marx, had little time for the family as an autonomous political agent. For him, the family, as other social institutions, was largely determined in its form and practice by the economic relations which underlay it.[11] The bourgeois family was irredeemably condemned by history, as was the bourgeoisie itself. The fact that Marx's own greatest affections and emotions were domestic ones and that his was very much a bourgeois family, though in dire economic straits for much of its existence, did not cause him to reflect at any length upon the place of the family in the historical process. Bourgeois families, according to him, were generally founded upon hypocrisy and reification, with wives being treated as the mere property of male heads of families. Once an 'era of social revolution' opened, new forms of cohabitation between adults and children would develop in the context of a collectivist society and of parity between the genders. Families as we know them were destined to disappear.

Marx's view of the family is, therefore, of some interest as a critique of Victorian domestic relations and as a vague blueprint for a future society, but it is of no help at all for our present task. It takes no account of the central importance of families as socialising agencies, as places which form character, association and opinion on a daily basis. At the risk of irritating profoundly Marx's more rigid admirers, it should be said that in modern capitalist societies families are politically at least as important as factories, and probably more so. They have a centrality which no other institution can match. They harbour secrets, memories and language that are theirs alone. Opinions expressed around a kitchen table, the reactions to the evening news on television, the last words whispered to a child at bedtime, attitudes and behaviour passed from one generation to another by gestures as much as by words, all these shape profoundly the way in which a family's members look at the world beyond the home and respond to its orders or suggestions.[12]

Every family is different and each has its own individuality and history. Yet there can be little doubt that under modern consumer capitalism most families, for the reasons I have outlined, are overwhelmingly conformist (in Mill's sense of the term) and self-absorbed. They are not, by and large, producers of active and dissenting individuals, nor do they contribute anything but a minimum part of their extraordinary energy and creativity to a public democratic sphere. It is as if, by a sleight of hand, they have been separated from politics. How to break through that separation, to release some of those energies so that they could contribute to the reinvention of democracy, is probably the greatest rebus of modern politics.

I believe that such a transformation can be achieved only by what I would like to call *a system of connections*. Families need to be connected to civil society by means of thriving networks of autonomous associations. These, in turn, need to be linked to the organs of democratic government by new forms of democracy which combine representative and participatory features. In each of the three spheres – families, civil society and the democratic state – active and dissenting individuals would play key roles of connection. It is they who shake families out of their passivity, who through their intelligence and self-discipline help civil society to grow, who take an active part in democratic politics but do not conceive of it as a separate sphere for their own self-aggrandisement. Each of the three spheres is dependent on the other. There can be no stable civil society without the active support and encouragement of the democratic state. Nor can democratic politics renew itself without the active support and control of civil-society associations. Nor, finally, can either of them prosper if they do not have their ideas firmly rooted in families which aspire to be, in Mill's magnificent words, 'real schools in the virtues of freedom'. The remainder of this book is dedicated to the exploration of these ideas, with special reference to the contribution that can be made to this interlocking process by different forms of democratic practice.

# 4

## THE CHALLENGE OF CIVIL SOCIETY

Before proceeding further I would like quickly to clear up a misunderstanding which may already have arisen in some readers' minds. I am not advocating a type of hyper-activism, in which individuals are called upon to sacrifice their own private and family lives, and where the reasons of the private sphere gradually lose out to those of the public one. A Jacobin model of citizenship of this sort, strongly tilted towards the constant presence of men in the public sphere, has little to offer modern democratic politics. It is likely to enforce rigid separations, most often along gender lines, rather than to establish a system of connections. Families, civil society and the democratic state need to exist in a mutually reinforcing equilibrium. The quest for the ideal forms of that equilibrium cannot begin with the sacrifice of one element to another. Still less can it begin, as in communist societies, with the enforced subordination of two of the elements – family and civil society – to an over-powerful third, the state.

What I have in mind instead is a more restrained and sensitive view of the active citizen. The modern active and dissenting citizen, whether woman or man, is no Jacobin, but seeks instead, often with difficulty, a balance for the different parts of her or his life. Home and family life are one fundamental section of daily experience. But so too is participation in civil society.

Few terms in modern politics are more frequently and loosely employed than civil society. Its most common usage today is as a description of both an analytical space and of an associational practice. As an analytical space, civil society is a vast intermediate area between private life, the economy and the state. Civil society relates to families, to markets and to governments, but is separate from them. As associational practice, civil society is characterised by a myriad of self-forming and self-dissolving voluntary organisations, circles, clubs, rank-and-file networks, social movements and so on. Some of these may acquire great stability and force, for example international organisations such as Amnesty International.[13] Others, the majority, may have much briefer lives, formed at a local level in a moment of enthusiasm and general mobilisation, but destined soon to disappear.

However, civil society cannot be defined only in terms of *analytical space* and *associational practice*. It has also always had strong *normative content*, though the precise nature of that content is bound to be modified from one generation to another. The German historian Jürgen Kocka has suggested convincingly that its origins are in the European Enlightenment, and that the project of civil society, however variegated and developed over time, is still an Enlightenment one.[14] In contemporary terms civil society can be said to harbour specific ambitions within the general condition of modern democracy: to foster the diffusion of power rather than its concentration, to use peaceful rather than violent means, to work for gender equality and social equity, to build horizontal solidarities rather than vertical loyalties, to encourage tolerance and inclusion, to stimulate debate and autonomy of judgement rather than conformity and obedience.

Civil society defined in this triple way – analytical space, associational practice and normative values – has witnessed an extraordinary growth in democratic countries in the last twenty years; not just in its Scandinavian heartlands, but in many Latin American countries and on the Indian sub-continent as well. In the same period, extended *international* networks of non-governmental organisations (NGOs) have been created, which in spite of great difficulties are in the process of giving substance to the concept of a global civil society. Since 2001 the *Global Civil Society Yearbook*, an initiative of the Centres for Civil Society at the London School of Economics and of the University of California, Los Angeles, has been regular testimony to these developments.

It would be fair to state that this great expansion of participatory forms within society, at local, national and international levels, was not something that was foreseen or conceptualised very fully by either Mill or Marx. If we consider Mill first, there can be no doubting his belief in the importance of associationism in society. In 1840, commenting on Tocqueville's *Democracy in America*, a work which underlined the vital role of self-organised groups of every sort in America's youthful democracy, Mill noted how in England too it was 'in the power of *combined action* that the progress of Democracy has been the most gigantic'. And what he had in mind were political unions, anti-slavery societies and the like, 'to say nothing of the less advanced but already powerful organisation of the working classes'. But Mill immediately qualified their role, and in a sense demoted it: 'These various associations are not the machinery of democratic combination, but the occasional weapons which that spirit forges as it needs them.' The real transformative agents were others. First of all, newspapers: 'It is by these that the people learn, it may truly be said, their own wishes, and through these that they declare them.' And secondly, railways. Together, 'newspapers and railroads are solving the problem of bringing the democracy of England to vote, like that of Athens, simultaneously in one *agorà*'.[15]

Not only was this a very optimistic, and in the event unfounded, view of the role of the press and transport in forming a democratic public. It also, crucially, treated civil-society associationism as an 'occasional weapon' rather than as a necessary and vital underlying structure in the creation of democracy. And in his *Considerations on Representative Government*, popular participation on a local level appears to be confined to minor actions such as jury service or serving on a parish council. Mill thus appears to have a splendid idea of individuality, but to lack a theorised organisational context, outside of the governing elites, in which to place these individuals. He wants the people to control government, but he gives them few or no instruments to do so.

In her important recent work on Mill Nadia Urbinati, though deeply sympathetic to his figure and his ideas, is led to ask a series of anguished questions about the role he ascribes to popular participation: 'What role do ordinary citizens play in Mill's "talking" government? Are they not as silent as those of Harrington's *Oceana*? In Mill's model, don't the people select their "betters" to speak in their place as a remedy for their own incompetence?'[16]

It has to be said that this is a deficiency not just of Mill, but of much liberal thought. Constant, as we have seen, exhorted citizens to 'an active and constant surveillance' over their representatives, but was entirely vague as to the instruments to be employed. Nor is the question only that of *control* over representatives, political parties, bureaucracy, etc. It is also one of *contribution*: what citizens can offer, through the associations of civil society, to a vital and creative democratic public sphere. If a 'system of connections' is to function, it cannot do so in the absence of any proper theorisation of the role to be played by civil society.

This absence in liberal thought can be partially explained in historical terms. For much of the nineteenth century liberal and indeed much of socialist thought ascribed an exalted, but also exaggerated potential to parliamentary assemblies. Mill himself was no exception. In his *Considerations on Representative Government* he wrote:

> The Parliament has an office . . . to be at once the nation's Committee of Grievances, and its Congress of Opinions; an arena in which not only the general opinion of the nation, but that of every section of it, and as far as possible of every eminent individual whom it contains, can produce itself in full light and challenge discussion; where every person in the country may count upon finding somebody who speaks his mind, as well or better than he could speak it himself.[17]

More than 150 years later we are entitled, I think, to take a more realistic, even jaundiced, view of the capabilities of parliaments, and to recognise the necessity in modern democracy for representative and participatory democracy to be actively and consistently intertwined.

Did Marxism go further than liberalism in this area? Marx himself, so deeply committed to the radical utopian disjuncture of socialist revolution, has little to say about self-organisation during the pre-revolutionary period, and even less to say about it after the revolution has taken place. He certainly believed in association, as his militancy in the First International and other organisations shows clearly. But the whole thrust of his thought pointed in another direction – to the *class* which would make the revolution, to its long struggle to become a class not just 'in itself' but 'for itself', to that final paroxysm of capital in which the proletariat, 'a class always increasing in numbers, and disciplined, united, organised by the very mechanism of the process of capitalist production itself', finally expropriates the bourgeoisie which has for so long exploited it.[18]

Among the Marxists who followed in his wake, it was undoubtedly Antonio Gramsci who thought hardest and longest about organisation within civil society. In a famous passage in the *Prison Notebooks* he explained how the conquest of power in the West would be not the result of a frontal assault upon the state, but the product of a long, slow and tenacious 'war of position' to conquer what he called the 'powerful system of fortresses and earthworks of civil society'.[19] This slow, molecular expansion of cultural and organisational influence seemed for a long time to offer an alternative road to power for communism in the West.

However, Gramsci was very much a child of his time, not only because of the First World War metaphors that he employed, but also in his admiration for Lenin and, eventually, for the Leninist party. After the debacle of the period 1920–26, Gramsci was ever more convinced of the necessary and all-embracing role of a powerful political organisation, the 'Modern Prince' as he called it, an expression with obvious Machiavellian overtones, and whose collective incarnation was the Communist Party. It was the Party that had to incorporate and organise within itself all that moved in civil society. The Leninist party once again makes its appearance as the all-powerful subject of politics, and even in Gramsci's humane version of the communist world the space for a creative and critical civil society is strictly limited.

~

So far I have presented modern civil society in very benign terms. It is as well to end this section with a more sober view.

The organisations of civil society have many shortcomings. Often their very informality and fluidity, so attractive at one level, are a severe drawback at another. In the absence of formal rules, it is easy for individuals to take advantage of their positions as charismatic founding figures or the like, and attempt to control organisations or to place themselves beyond criticism. Sadly, the individual self-control and self-discipline, the humility, imagination and scepticism so eloquently invoked by Mill, are often lacking in both leaders and led in civil society. And if both internal and external democratic constraints are lacking, then an association's prospects are not good. Indeed, it is far easier for a hierarchical organisation to prosper than it is for one dedicated to the principles of horizontal solidarities and the diffusion of power. To build civil society requires peculiar qualities of patience and tenacity as well as an innate culture of democracy. Often one or more of these qualities is absent.

Furthermore, there is the problem of representation. Who exactly do civil-society organisations represent? And how is this to be ascertained? Grandiloquent names may conceal little more than individual ambition. In the international arena, more than one national government has had recourse to the invention of false NGOs, which pretend to be part of civil society but represent only that government's particular interests. These are called GONGOS: government operated non-governmental organisations.

All these drawbacks and shortcomings should not be swept quietly under the carpet by the supporters of civil society. They should be brought out into the open so that they can be properly discussed. Too much of the literature on civil society has unwelcome gung-ho overtones. Civil-society organisations, even in Scandinavia, need clear codes of conduct to help frame behaviour and to help people understand what they can expect and what is expected of them. There is a difficult equilibrium to be established between informality and rules of procedure, spontaneity and regular democratic consultation. It is not easy to get this balance right.

However, even with their actual and often considerable shortcomings, the organisations of civil society – at local, national and even international levels – are playing an invaluable role, one which in political terms goes beyond both Marx and Mill. They are trying to pull individuals, at least for some of the time, out of over-privatised lives, to create widening circles of critical, informed and participating citizens from all parts of the political spectrum, and to instigate dialogue with politicians on some basis of equality and mutual respect. They are trying to connect. But do the politicians, in their separate and privileged sphere, want to connect with them?

# 5

## DELIBERATIVE DEMOCRACY

The present period has strong points of contact with the 1970s, and the lessons of that decade should serve as a warning to us. All over Europe at that time there were widespread mobilisations for the extension of democracy in various spheres – in local government by means of neighbourhood councils, in the workplace through factory councils and other forms of shop-floor representation, in schools through the greater involvement of parents, and so on. So great was the pressure for change that the Italian political philosopher Norberto Bobbio noted 'an ascending power' which was spreading to 'various spheres of civil society'. He continued: 'Seen from this angle I believe that it is justified to talk of a genuine turning-point in the evolution of democratic institutions which can be summed up in a simple formula: from the democratisation of the state to the democratisation of society'.[20]

Unfortunately, no such transformation took place. The mountain gave birth to a molehill. This failure can be explained in part by the changing balance of forces at the end of the 1970s – the decline of the social movements of the previous years, the re-establishment of employers' control and discipline in the factories, and above all the rise of an all-conquering international ideology, that of neo-liberalism. But it was also due in no small part to the incapacity and unwillingness of left-wing political parties to channel the great pressure from below into new forms of governance, to rethink democratic participation and to break out of a model of politics in which their own influence was fortified within the state but democracy as a whole was not enriched.

It would be good not to make the same mistakes a second time round. All over Europe a new rhetoric is circulating which stresses the need for 'the empowerment of ordinary people'. The European Union, in various communications and programmes, does not hesitate to underline expressions such as 'partnership', 'citizen involvement', 'participation'. However, unless participation assumes solid, workable and constant forms, then all talk about 'empowerment' will be little more than hot air.

What might these forms look like? The recent discussion and experimentation in the realm of 'deliberative' democracy help us along the road of innovation and renovation. But we must be careful to distinguish, and not to embrace uncritically every experiment and idea that shelters under that broad umbrella. In particular I would like to introduce two yardsticks, crucial to the argument of this book, by which deliberative practices may be measured. The first has been briefly mentioned above: the degree to which they contribute to creating widening circles of critical, informed and participating citizens, who debate with politicians and administrators on some basis of equality and mutual respect. The second, closely linked, is how far deliberative practices contribute to changing the way politicians themselves behave and how they view their prerogatives and duties. The first has to do with the growth of civil society, the second with the cultural transformation of the political class. In the absence of one or both of these yardsticks, it is unlikely that deliberative experimentation will contribute much to the long-term renewal of democracy. In other words, the parameters of politics have to change significantly, with the previously separate political sphere becoming, at the very least, more porous and receptive. Mill and Marx, representative and participatory democracy, civil society and local government good practices, have to be genuinely and variously *combined*.

To put the matter in its most simple and brutal form, nothing will be gained by politicians offering the old model of representative democracy with a sprinkling of consultation or the odd public assembly or citizens' jury thrown in for good measure. But that is what they are doing, for the most part, all over Europe, and their actions are little more than hoodwinking. The independent report on the state of British democracy, *Power to the People*, supported by the Joseph Rowntree Trust and published in March 2006, was quite explicit on this point: 'The evidence received by us . . . is that popular cynicism towards public consultation is very strong. The process is widely regarded as meaningless, in that it is often unclear how a consultation process can influence final decisions taken by officials or representatives.'[21]

~

Deliberative democracy derives its name from the dual meaning in English of 'deliberation' – both to discuss and to decide. Citizens will be called into a deliberative arena not just to debate among themselves or with politicians, but to play some significant role in the decision-making process. The notion has at its core the idea of making policy by involving all those who will be affected by a decision, or their representatives.[22] The method employed is structured debate in a collaborative context, founded on adequate information and a plurality of opinions, with clear time limits set for reaching decisions. Ideally, deliberative arenas help citizens to feel informed and involved, not isolated, ignorant and powerless. They help politicians and administrators to govern better and to bridge the gap which all too often separates them from society.

Deliberative democracy boasts a number of qualities. In the first place, it has the capacity, though not the certainty, of producing better decisions, because in the course of discussion problems come to be redefined, politicians become better informed of citizens' opinions, and new mediations and solutions are proposed. Second, deliberation can enhance the legitimacy of decisions, because they are the fruit not of a small isolated group of decision-makers, but of a plurality of interested parties, some of whom may not agree with the final decision but all of whom recognise the legitimacy of the procedure that has taken place. Third, and most importantly for our purposes, deliberation strengthens civic virtues, because it teaches people to listen, educates them in public matters and often builds trust among them.[23]

Once again it is Mill, not Marx, who anticipates this sort of democratic discourse. In *Considerations on Representative Government* he wrote: 'What can be done better by a body than by any individual is deliberation. When it is necessary, or important, to secure hearing and consideration to many conflicting opinions, a deliberative body is indispensable.'[24] Mill also underlined the 'learning function' of deliberation. It was quite wrong, he stressed, to consider one's own opinion 'an absolute certainty'. Listening to and debating the opinions of others helped citizens to grow and established a proper link between 'talking and doing'.[25]

Yet Mill stops short here, and not for the first time. In his work the principles of deliberation are not applied to a wide number of arenas so that decision-making, in one form or another, could become the habit and prerogative of citizens. On the contrary, he felt strongly that most decisions were best taken by a single expert. His underlying fear of the mass of uneducated people exercising too much power in modern democracy – of the tyranny of an ill-informed majority – is never far from the surface. Deliberation, in his scheme of government, was best confined to Parliament, to the assembly of representatives elected by proportional representation. And even at this level, as we have seen, there existed for him a radical division of tasks, between 'talking and doing'. Parliament 'talked', and it was very valuable that it did so. But it was a non-elected executive of competent experts that 'did'.

# 6

## LOCAL GOVERNMENT AND
## THE RENEWAL OF DEMOCRACY

Let me begin this time with Marx. Differently from Mill, he never wrote a book about democracy, and the historical model of local government that he chose as his guide lasted, as we have seen, just seventy-one days. Had the Paris Commune of 1871 survived, it would certainly have encountered significant problems of democratic principle and organisation which would have had to have been resolved. One such was the necessary separation of powers and the balance between them; another the vulnerability of delegates (as opposed to representatives) to constant recall and a consequent risk of lack of continuity; another still the complicated nature of a new French republic based upon a federation of communes.

However, two things transpire very clearly from Marx's scattered comments on democratic forms. The first is the great thrust in his writings towards egalitarianism, conceived of not just in terms of civil rights (the original *égalité* of the revolution of 1789), but in terms of structures of privilege and power. In his pamphlet on the Commune, 'The Civil War in France', prepared for the General Council of the First International, he writes of the need for 'doing away with the state hierarchy altogether and replacing the haughty masters of the people by always removable servants, a mock responsibility by a real responsibility, as they act continuously under public supervision'.[26] Accountability, accessibility, ease of substitution, parity of economic retribution – these are some of the basic qualities that Marx seeks out for democratic institutions and administration, and which have long since been lost in modern democracy.

At the same time, and this is the second point, he writes in Utopian terms in 'The Jewish Question' and elsewhere of the way in which the rebus of modern politics will be resolved only when the 'real individual man' succeeds in resuming the 'abstract [political] citizen' back into himself, so that politics and society are once again *united*; 'only then will human emancipation be completed'.[27] There is perhaps something disturbingly holistic and final about this political dream. It seems much more likely that democracy will always be about pluralism and dissent, without ever arriving at perfection. But the thrust of Marx's argument is clear enough and entirely welcome. Nowadays, the need to reconnect the political sphere with society, to overcome a separation that at times seems an abyss, is felt very strongly.

By comparison, Mill on local government is rather disappointing. Here, if anywhere, we might have expected his great love of Athens to have been translated into innovatory institutional proposals as well as elements of everyday politics. Instead in the chapter of his *Considerations* dedicated to 'Local representative bodies', we get nothing of the sort. He starts, as usual, with an impeccable statement of principle: 'Two points require an equal degree of our attention: how the local business can best be done; and how its transaction can be made most instrumental to the nourishment of public spirit and the development of intelligence.'[28] But in what follows he seems strangely bereft of ideas. He notes that in the case of local government citizens do not only elect; many of them also have the chance of being elected, and 'many, either by selection or rotation, fill one or other of the numerous local executive offices'.[29] However, even in Mill's time this last statement could only have been true of a very small group of citizens and by adopting a very limited definition of citizenship. Contemporary local democracy boasts no system of rotation in offices. All over Europe the 'numerous local executive offices', such as the directors of municipal services, are filled time and again by the party faithful in preference to competent citizens without party allegiances.

Worse is to come in Mill's account of the guiding principles of local government. On the local as on the national level, he advises the granting of a plural vote to certain categories of citizens. However, at a local level he is more inclined for this electoral elite to depend on 'a mere money qualification'. Looked at through twenty-first-century eyes, his explanation has something of the perverse about it: 'for the honest and frugal dispensation of money forms so much a larger part of the business of the local, than of the national body, that there is more justice as well as policy in allowing a greater proportional influence to those who have a larger money interest at stake'.[30] Mill appears here to be advocating a patrimonial version of local democracy, wherein power is concentrated in the hands of those who have most money.

~

In the light of the discussion above, it is now possible to turn, if all too briefly, to various contemporary proposals for participatory democracy at the local level. It is immediately apparent that very many of them move in a positive direction, and that at least one goes beyond Marx and Mill in proposing a quite novel combination of representative and participative democracy. However, it is as well to be clear from the start that they are not all equal, in the sense that they do not all satisfy in equal measure the two yardsticks that I proposed in the previous section. What follows is a typology which necessarily contains elements of hierarchy within it.

Experiments in, and proposals for, deliberative democracy have taken a very wide number of forms – there are the German *Planungszelle* (planning cells), American and British citizens' juries, electronic town meetings, consensus conferences, James Fishkin's proposal in the United States for a national deliberation day, Chicago's experimentation in citizens' governance in policing and public education, the e.thePeople website, Danish empowerment of parents in primary schools, and so on.[31]

In trying to distinguish between them, we can isolate at least two major groups. The first is that which has at its core a process of selection, either random or controlled. A citizens' jury, for example, as its name implies, is a microcosm of a given community brought together, usually by local administrators, to deliberate upon an issue of public interest. In order to achieve a faithful cross section of the community, jurors are 'stratified' by age, education, gender, geographic location, ethnicity and sometimes politics. Between twelve and twenty-four citizens usually compose the group. It receives information on the topic under discussion from expert witnesses, and its discussions are steered by trained facilitators. The jury sits for between one and five days, and its findings, which are made public, are usually presented as non-binding recommendations to local administrators and politicians. Jurors are usually paid for their services ($150 a day in the United States), but we should find nothing scandalous about that. In ancient Athens citizens were also paid for their presence in the *agorà* on a daily basis. Between 1996 and 2005 some 230 citizens' juries were convened in Britain, the USA, Australia and a number of other countries.[32] German planning cells are similar, but are often run concurrently or in series, so as to include more citizens in the process.

A similar though numerically more ambitious enterprise is the electronic town meeting. Here hundreds, sometimes even thousands, of citizens are brought together for a more limited period of time, at most a day, to deliberate on an issue of public importance. Publicity and media coverage of the event, given its size, is likely to be much greater than that accorded to a citizens' jury. Controlled sampling is again the method most often adopted to ensure that a proper cross section of the local population is involved, but sometimes room is made for representatives of civil-society groups. The town meeting has a complex structure designed to give all participants the feeling that they are contributing to the formulation of policy. A large number of small groups, ten to twelve strong, demographically and socially diverse in their composition, meet around tables and deliberate animatedly. The fruits of their discussion are transmitted by computer to a central database, and members of a 'theme team' distil them into key themes or messages. These are then presented back to the meeting as a whole, and a series of policy indicators emerges by the end of the day. Once again, these are usually non-binding recommendations.

One of the most spectacular town meetings took place in New York in July 2002. Under discussion was the redevelopment of the former World Trade Center site, devastated by the terrorist attack of 11 September 2001. More than 200 members of the media followed the deliberations of a 5,000-strong town meeting which was highly critical of the development plans submitted to it. The meeting wanted less density of office space, a twenty-four-hour community centre in downtown Manhattan and a more mixed use of the Ground Zero space. The meeting received intense, if brief, publicity; politicians and planners promised to do better and a few of the meeting's ideas were eventually incorporated into new plans.[33]

In assessing this first group of participatory practices, I want to underline initially what I see as their advantages. The most significant is their ability to involve members of the general public who otherwise would be highly unlikely to become involved in public policy issues. Random or controlled selection usually ensures the presence of citizens whom civil-society groups, at least as at present constituted, have great difficulty in contacting. Low-income families and individuals with few educational qualifications are the target group here. Secondly, the process of participating – whether in a town meeting or planning group or citizens' jury – is in itself usually highly attractive, giving citizens a real sense that they are making a useful contribution. Third, public attention can be drawn to specific issues and viewpoints that might otherwise remain in obscurity, especially by large assemblies like electronic town meetings. Deliberative arenas of this sort can break through, at least temporarily, to the world of the politicians, and strongly encourage them to see a specific problem in a different light. Some commentators have talked about helping politicians and administrators to overcome their 'blind spots'.

However, there are also limitations. The 'one-off' nature of these events, especially costly and complex occasions such as electronic town meetings, robs them of an essential element – that of *continuity*. The cost of convening a citizens' jury is estimated at £16–30,000; that of a town meeting over £200,000. Participants may want to go on being involved, but they are offered no ongoing structures or instruments to enable them to do so. Nor are they likely (*pace* Mill) to be 'selected' more than once, or to find a natural system of rotation being practised in the local sphere, whereby local political elites voluntarily draw back from power. Modern politicians at all levels are not renowned for their self-denying qualities.

Second, these sampling experiments show little sensibility to the particular importance of civil-society groups in renovating democracy. Often the opposite is true. I have heard civil-society groups being described as 'ranters', the 'usual crowd', a 'nuisance'. Active and dissenting citizens are rarely recognised by politicians, administrators or experts as a potentially precious resource for the renewal of a democratic public sphere. 'Ordinary' citizens are welcome, but those (often middle-class) who are already trying to do something about an issue are frequently regarded with suspicion or impatience.

Third, and perhaps most crucially, there are no mechanisms to ensure that politicians will actually implement any of the proposals that these 'random sample' groups produce. Indeed, their one-off nature weakens this possibility. The newspapers may be full of a town meeting for a day or two, but what happens after that? Lack of follow-up and continuity may well, at the end of the day, leave planners and politicians a more or less free hand. One long-term American survey of the success rate of citizens' juries concluded sadly that 'recommendations to agencies or local governments failed to have much impact'.[34]

If we return for a moment to the two yardsticks that I introduced earlier, we can see that these experiments do little to satisfy either of them. They contribute marginally, if at all, to creating widening circles of critical, informed and participating citizens, who communicate with politicians and administrators on some basis of equality and mutual respect. Nor do they do much to change the way politicians view themselves and their prerogatives. At the crucial moment when the consultation is over, the electronic gadgets have been put back in their boxes and the administrators have to decide, there is little in institutional terms to *compel* them to respect the views that have been expressed by a random sample of citizens. Participatory models of this sort are attractive and innovative but they do not really answer our need to reinvent the connection between participation and representation. They are rather auxiliary, consultative mechanisms for representative democracy.

~

A second group of participatory practices differs from the first because, rather than relying on random sampling, it operates an 'open-door' policy and tries to involve ever-widening circles of the population of a locality or territory in decision-making processes. Here the deliberative process is not auxiliary or subsidiary, but tries to combine representative and participative democracy.

I can illustrate this experimentation best by considering briefly the case of Porto Alegre in Brazil. It is an example which may be well known to some readers, but its key elements have not often been discussed adequately, and quite a lot of wild claims have been made for it. At first sight, the city of Porto Alegre, with 22 per cent of its 1.3 million population still living in shanty towns or other 'irregular settlements' in the year 2000, with its mass poverty and (until recently) mass illiteracy, would seem an unlikely place for a complicated experimentation in combined democracy. If, as Mill suggests in his *Considerations on Representative Government*, literacy and a long-term learning process are to be considered determining causal conditions for participating in democracy, then Porto Alegre would be a non-starter.

Instead over a period of over fifteen years – not the seventy-odd days of the Paris Commune – an impressive tradition of popular deliberation has been created, and not at the margins of the local government system but at its core – the control over the city's budget, and the way in which scarce resources are to be equitably distributed. The process by which these priorities are established and then enacted has come to be known as the 'participatory budget' (Orçamento Participativo, or OP). A leading role in promoting and sustaining the process has been played by the political party at present in power in Brazil – the Partido dos Trabalhadores or Workers' Party.[35]

The first thing to note about the 'participatory budget' is its annual character. Different parts of it take place regularly on certain dates. The 'participatory budget' is not an open-ended discussion or a mere consultation, but a series of decisions made according to a seasonal timetable available to all. Thus in March a series of micro-level preparatory reunions are held all over the city. In April and May there are territorial and thematic assemblies which vote the priorities for the coming year, and the election of forty-eight delegates from these assemblies to the Budget Council. At the end of this first phase the requests of the citizens are handed solemnly to the mayor and Municipal Council.

The Budget Council meets from September onwards – administrators, municipal councillors and the elected delegates from the assemblies – and together they thrash out a programme. The participatory budget, which is not an official government institution, and is governed more by 'soft' than 'hard' legislation, is then adopted by the mayor at the end of the year. The whole process is aided and facilitated by twenty coordinators from the city's Coordination Committee for Relations with the Community.[36]

This is only a bald summary of a complex process. A number of points stand out. The final decisions and responsibility rest with those elected by representative democracy, but only after a process of the intertwining of the two democracies that lasts a year. Secondly, there has been a steadily increasing number of citizens who participate – from just 1,300 in 1989 to 31,300 in 2002. Their social and gender composition is also revealing, with a clear majority of women and poor people taking part. A significant number also come from the city's ethnic minorities, who until recently had been forbidden even to shop in the same supermarkets as white Brazilians.[37]

However – and this is absolutely crucial – the 30,000 people who take part are only a small minority of the city's adult population. And if we look at other experiments in deliberative democracy, less extraordinary, but which harbour similar ambitions, we find much the same story. In Chicago, for instance, between 1997 and 2000 the city spent more than $1.5 million on media efforts to advertise citizen participation in community policing and public education governance. Even so, each month only about 5–6,000 residents attended beat meetings and school meetings in the whole of the city.[38]

It is quite clear, therefore, that participatory democracy of this sort, however precious, is a minority activity and cannot replace representative democracy, which for all its failings still involves well over half the adult population in a secret and formal process of voting. But the two can and indeed must meet, with the liberty of the ancients coming to the aid of that of the moderns. The power and responsibility of representatives are not negated or even diminished. They are, rather, modified, enriched and institutionally constrained by the deliberative and participatory activity that is taking place around them. And the crucial theoretical point regarding the relationship between the two – between representative and participatory democracy – is that *the activity of the second guarantees the quality of the first*. If it works well, deliberative democracy guarantees transparency, builds wider circles of decision-making and plays a crucial role in the formation of a small but expanding group of educated and active citizens with an ethic of public service in their very bones. In his mild way, Mill would have been surprised and enthusiastic about such an extension of democracy, while Marx would have noted in his explosive prose the analogies with the Paris Commune, though this time without the enemy at its very gates.

~

Let me briefly bring the story of Porto Alegre up to date. At the end of October 2004, the ruling Partido dos Trabalhadores (PT), which had been principally responsible for introducing and nurturing the participatory budget, was defeated at the local elections. A very broad twelve-party coalition headed by José Fogaça took power. The PT had become too accustomed to power, and Fogaça's appeals for democratic alternation and an end to 'one-party rule' proved effective, especially in appealing to more conservative, middle-class voters. However, it was highly significant that the new mayor insisted that he would continue the Orçamento Participativo, which he presented as a 'triumph of civil society' and a reflection of the city's 'associative capacity'.

The fate of this most novel example of empowered participatory democracy now hangs in the balance. On the one hand there exists room for optimism, given the roots that participative democracy has put down in the city. On the other, some expert commentators such as Daniel Chavez identify a watering-down process under way, and the need for a new mobilisation from Porto Alegre's civil society to defend the essential elements of the city's famous experiment in participatory democracy.[39]

Looking at Porto Alegre in a wider context, it has often been noted that it is a model difficult to imitate or to export. As Gianpaolo Baiocchi has pointed out, Porto Alegre stands apart from many other similar attempts in Brazil and Latin America, in terms of both the numbers involved and the amount of decision-making power devolved to popular mandate.[40] Attempts to introduce participatory budgets in Europe have so far met with mixed success.

One noteworthy experiment in the British context was the Harrow Open Budget Process, designed and managed by the Power Inquiry in association with the London Borough of Harrow. On a Sunday afternoon in March, 2005, 300 residents took part in six hours of deliberation, discussing and voting key priorities for the borough's 2006/2007 budget. The recruitment campaign for the deliberative assembly succeeded in ensuring the presence of a fair cross section of the community. At the end of the afternoon the participants elected an Open Budget Panel, whose main role was to keep an eye on the local politicians as they drew up the budget, and report back on the extent to which the assembly's priorities were being addressed.[41]

It is the ambitions and rigour of the Porto Alegre model that recommend it in the context of this book; that is, of 'returning to first principles', of trying to rethink democracy not merely in contingent or mechanical terms, nor primarily as a question of institutional engineering. If we return to the two yardsticks that I suggested earlier, the experience of Porto Alegre goes a long way to satisfying both. It has genuinely helped to create, year by year, widening circles of participating citizens, who have entered into a virtuous relationship with the administrators and politicians of the city. Families and neighbourhoods have been linked to civil-society associations and the local state in a continuous form.[42]

The deliberative practice of the OP has also helped to change the administrative culture of the city itself. The clientelism and corruption which is so marked a feature of Brazilian politics has been checked. Administrators and experts have not been left to their own deliberations, but forced to come out of their offices and explain in comprehensible language what they consider possible or impossible, and why. This, too, forms part of an invaluable Millian educative process for all concerned.

A last point. It has sometimes been suggested by experts in this field that there is no need to choose a single model of deliberative practice, nor establish a hierarchy among them. There is force in this argument, but also danger. It is clear that different practices are appropriate in different contexts, and that it may also be possible to combine practices. But a citizens' jury or a town meeting does seem to me to be qualitatively inferior in terms of democratic renewal to the sort of civil-society–state experimentation that has taken place at Porto Alegre. That difference should be clearly recognised. Furthermore, if all practices are presented as being equally significant, it is all too easy for lukewarm politicians to *substitute* a demanding process of renewal with something much less arduous. The 'ascending power' of which Norberto Bobbio talked is then channelled into limited solutions which are more auxiliary than others, and which have little momentum. In this way a repetition of the European experience in the 1970s is on the cards, with a great head of participative steam unable to push the locomotive of democracy more than a few metres along the track.[43] We should instead be clear about our overall objectives, in no way ashamed of their ambitions, and act accordingly.

PART 3

# 1

## ECONOMIC DEMOCRACY

Up until this point I have concentrated on democracy as a *political system*, but the causes of its present crisis are not, as we have seen, exclusively political. I need now to cast a wider net and consider other fields which bear upon our central problem. One of the most important of these is economics. Most of the literature on democracy, especially of liberal stamp, pretends that gross disparities of wealth and power between individual citizens in modern democracies have little bearing upon the quality of those democracies themselves. Quite the opposite is true. If citizens share equal rights in the political sphere, but are highly unequal in the economic one, then democracy is likely to be deeply flawed. Often older democracies are referred to as 'mature' ones. But perhaps 'over-ripe' would be a better term if, as in the case of the USA, they are characterised by such dubious mechanisms as unlimited electoral funding and corporate lobbying.[1]

It would be strange indeed to argue, as I have done, in favour of a system of political connections between families, civil society and the state, and then to leave economic relations unexamined and untouchable. Robert A. Dahl, one of the United States' most accomplished democratic theorists, is very clear about the necessary connection between the two spheres. He has gone as far as to claim that 'if democracy is justified in governing the state, then it must also be justified in governing economic enterprises; and to say that it is *not* justified in governing economic enterprises is to imply that it is not justified in governing the state'.[2]

In historical terms he asks a trenchant counterfactual question: 'Might not we Americans be different, if in the 1880s we had adopted self-governing enterprises [i.e. a system of economic democracy within firms] rather than corporate capitalism as the standard solution?'[3] The broadly based agrarian equality which had been the economic foundation of America's young democracy, and whose self-dependence and self-organisation had so aroused the enthusiasm of Tocqueville in the 1830s, no longer prevailed at the end of the nineteenth century. Hard questions should then have been posed about the socio-economic organisation of American urban life and its connections to the political system. They never were. As Dahl writes, 'Americans have never asked themselves steadily or in large numbers whether an alternative to corporate capitalism might be more consistent with their commitment to democracy.'[4]

∼

I want to begin my discussion by looking again at our two great Victorian thinkers, to see what light they shed upon this most intractable of problems. It would be fair to say that in this field Marx comes finally into his own. As we have seen, very early on in his intellectual development (1843–4) he had denounced a political system in which all men appeared to be politically free and equal, but in which they remained in reality profoundly divided by inequalities of income and differential access to power. Nearly thirty years later he welcomed the Paris Commune not only because 'the very existence of the Commune involved . . . local municipal liberty', but also because it was 'the political form at last discovered under which to *work out* the economical emancipation of labour'.[5]

For Marx, in other words, to embrace the model of the Paris Commune meant to recognise that political and economic democracy *could* and indeed *had* to march forward hand-in-hand. And little matter if in economic terms the Commune had done no more than abolish night working for bakers and had even left untouched in the centre of Paris the mansion of Adolphe Thiers, who was to be responsible for repressing the Communards with terrible savagery. Marx was convinced none the less that the highly egalitarian and participatory nature of the Commune's democratic public sphere would perforce, if it had survived, have carried it onto the terrain of economic democracy.

However, Marx's analysis goes beyond the historical events of which he was an impassioned witness. Above all in his *Economic and Philosophical Manuscripts* of 1844, he reflects profoundly upon man's alienation – though rarely and super-ficially, it has to be said, upon woman's. According to Marx, alienation was present in many different fields of human activity – religious, political, economic – but common to them all was the idea that man had forfeited to someone or something what was essential to his nature, or 'species-being' as Marx called it. Fundamentally, man had alienated the capacity of control over his own activities, of being the initiator of the historical process.

Nowhere was this truer than in labour under capitalist production. Here the worker was alienated in two different ways – first from the product of his labour, which assumed the physiognomy of an 'alien object that has power over him', rather than he having power over it.[6] Secondly, in the production process itself, where the worker had no control over his own time and his labour belonged to someone else: 'It is activity that is passivity, power that is weakness, procreation that is castration.'[7] The net result of these two processes was described by the young Marx with extraordinary brilliance and inimitable force:

> Thus the worker only feels at home outside his work and in his work he feels a stranger. He is at home when he is not working and when he works he is not at home . . . the more value he creates, the more valueless and worthless he becomes, the more formed the product the more deformed the worker, the more civilised the product, the more barbaric the worker, the more powerful the work, the more powerless becomes the worker . . . When alienated labour tears from man the object of his production, it also tears from him his species-life, the real objectivity of his species, and turns the advantage he has over animals into a disadvantage in that his inorganic body, nature, is torn from him.[8]

Marx's path-breaking analysis of alienation in early capitalism and, it must be added, of alienation in much of global capitalism today, is not accompanied at any stage in his long intellectual career by a detailed programme of how economic and political democracy could steadily and fruitfully combine.

His solution to what he called the riddle of history was much more cathartic and impatient. It was revolution – a deeply romantic political category if ever there was one. For Marx as for many others, revolution is the celebration of the force of a single, sublime historical moment. In Marx's case, it was proletarian revolution that would finally restore man to his species-being.

At the heart of proletarian revolution lay the abolition of private property. Private property, wrote Marx in a passage that bears directly upon today's consumerism, 'has made us so stupid and narrow-minded that an object is only ours when we have it, when it exists as capital for us or when we directly possess, eat, drink, wear, inhabit it, etc., in short when we use it'.[9] Only by overcoming such endless proprietary attitudes could man become a truly social being; only then would human self-alienation come to an end; only then could 'the real re-appropriation of the human essence by and for man' take place.[10] And even if, as we saw in the Prologue to this book, Marx came to believe that in certain countries workers could seize power and make their own history by peaceful means, he never doubted that the nature of the coming revolution lay in the forcible abolition of private property. Ways of making the revolution could vary, but its economic essence could not.

Marx, then, offers no specific prescriptions for the way in which economic democracy could be organised, but he does present an extraordinary analysis of workers' alienation under capitalism, and a cathartic vision of the necessary political framework for its overcoming.

~

Mill is very different, though his points of contact with Marx are surprisingly frequent. Unlike very many liberals he did not choose to skate over the economic exploitation of the great majority of the world's population, or pretend that the mechanism of 'the rising tide of capitalism which will lift all boats' was the only feasible long-term economic strategy. On the contrary, he denounced vehemently the gross economic inequalities of modern society, and in language that was not that far from Marx's:

> Notwithstanding all that has been done, and all that seems
> likely to be done, in the extension of franchises, a few are born

to great riches, and the many to a penury, made only more grating by contrast. No longer enslaved or made dependent by force of law, the great majority are so by force of poverty; they are still chained to a place, to an occupation, and to conformity with the will of an employer, and debarred by the accident of birth both from the enjoyments, and from the mental and moral advantages, which others inherit without exertion and independently of desert. That this is an evil equal to almost any of those against which mankind have hitherto struggled, the poor are not wrong in believing.[11]

Was this a necessary evil? The poor, continues Mill, will be told that it is but they should not believe it. Time and again in human history, Mill argued in a typically anti-conformist passage, the 'opinions of mankind . . . have tended to consecrate existing facts, and to declare what did not yet exist, either pernicious or impracticable'. But established opinion was there to be overcome. 'The working classes', wrote Mill, 'are entitled to claim that the whole field of social institutions should be re-examined, and every question considered as if it now arose for the first time.'[12]

Written at the end of his life, these words of Mill seem to bring him very close to the socialist camp, if not to Marx himself. However, we should not exaggerate this consonance. The passion with which Marx, and indeed many nineteenth-century socialists such as Louis Blanc, with whom Mill corresponded for years, denounced the burgeoning system of capitalism do not find a correspondence in Mill himself. There is a distinction to be made here in terms of both attitude and content. Mill recognises the great social injustices all around him, he sympathises deeply with those who suffer under them, but he is distant from them. He hopes and works for the lower classes' social and cultural redemption, but so that they might one day be his equals, and as such take in hand the government of society. Marx, on the other hand, is deeply involved, not only analytically but also emotionally, with a class which has 'a universal character because of its universal suffering'.[13] He is not of that class, but by birth rather than by choice, and he is convinced that the proletariat is destined by history to redeem mankind.

These are very different subjective attitudes which find their counterpart in differing interpretations of the general historical direction of capitalism. For Marx capitalism is doomed: by its own internal economic mechanisms, by the falling rate of profit, by its ever greater concentration of firms, by the creation of its own 'gravedigger', the proletariat. For Mill, on the other hand, capitalism's downward trend is by no means clear cut. In certain areas conditions are improving, not getting worse. Wages do not have a general tendency to diminish. Pressure of population is a great but not an increasing evil. Competition is not only destructive but also beneficial. As for private property, it is 'not some one thing, identical throughout history and incapable of alteration, but is variable like all other creations of the human mind'.[14] Property should not be regarded as sacrosanct at all costs, especially when it stands in the way of the public good. But nor should its abolition be regarded as the key to human emancipation.

From the above discussion it is obvious that Mill has little time for revolution as a political project. He is a thoroughgoing reformist. As such, he champions the rights of trade unions to defend the working classes and to increase their influence. He also, as I mentioned in the Prologue to this book, believed workers' cooperatives to be the desirable future form of organisation for industrial production. But when it comes to the question that most interests us here, the connection between economic and political democracy, the creation of a broad parity of resources and power in the economic sphere to correspond to the political equality that democracy alone can offer, then Mill is rather more silent than Marx. His political thought maintains the classic liberal distinction between the political and the economic spheres. The political representation of the working classes will come about through the extension of the franchise, their economic amelioration through trade unions and cooperatives. But it is not clear how, if at all, the two will fruitfully combine.

~

What is very striking about today's discussions of economic democracy is how paltry they are in comparison with the mid-nineteenth-century debates which I have just outlined. Mill may be no Leveller, but he is a giant of social and economic reform when compared with his neo-liberal epigones. Nowadays we are a very long way indeed from any form of economic democracy. Indeed, we have clearly gone backwards, in some areas dramatically so.

There are three principal ways of defining economic democracy. The first, and most radical, is that of Marx: it consists in the revolutionary expropriation of the capitalist class, and the establishment of workers' control in the factories. This is a political model, as I tried to show briefly in Part I of this book, which exercised an enormous fascination for both European workers and intellectuals during the great part of the twentieth century, but it has not led in historical terms to greater democracy, either political or economic, rather to less.

The second, which we find most clearly present in the history of social democracy, defines economic democracy primarily in terms of increased workers' welfare rights and their greater share of overall income. Mature and responsible social democracies like those in Scandinavia have made great efforts to limit gross disparities of income and wealth, and have accompanied these with the creation of strong citizens' social rights. In general, European welfare states, by making a wide range of insurance, health and educational services available to citizens, have pushed forward the boundaries of this sort of economic democracy.[15] The extraordinary day of 5 July 1948, when millions of British citizens applied for free spectacles from the newly born National Health Service, must count as one of the great moments of European social reform.[16] But we should be careful not to exaggerate the *democratic* nature of such measures. However precious and essential they are, these are reforms that descend from on high towards a grateful but largely passive and atomised citizenship.

The third definition of economic democracy is the one on which I wish to concentrate here. It corresponds to the type of political participation which I have described for Porto Alegre and shares, we might say, the same aspirations. It has to do with greater democracy and empowerment at the workplace, the possibility for those who work in an institution, factory or service industry to make their voice heard and be part of a decision-making process. Active, dissenting citizens cannot just be present as a reforming movement within civil society and political institutions; they must also, in ways yet to be defined, carry these same democratic values into their daily work experience. The two spheres, economic and political, cannot be simply hermetically sealed one from the other.

In the world of neo-liberalism and flexible contracts of three weeks or three months, and of increasingly arbitrary employer power, it may seem blasphemous or at the very least antiquated to mention such things. They are certainly out of fashion. But as European citizens we would make a grave mistake to forget the considerable tradition that exists in our recent history of reflection and action on this issue – from Gramsci's *Ordine Nuovo* to the Italian factory councils of 1969 onwards; from the French Catholic trade union experiments in the 1970s in *autogestion* to Rudolf Meidner's striking proposals in Sweden in 1975 for employee investment funds.[17]

Let me just take two of these examples and illustrate them a little more, in order to give a better idea of what economic democracy might mean in practice. The first is to do with participatory activity, the second with the structural modification of property rights. In Italy in the 1970s the creation of factory councils and of a network of shop-floor delegates – by 1973 there were 16,000 councils and more than 150,000 delegates – served both to strengthen the presence of the trade unions vis-à-vis the employers, and to connect them more firmly with rank-and-file workers. Differently from the earlier Gramscian experience of 1919–20, the system of councils and delegates was not a minority movement, but came to be adopted by the Italian trade union movement as a whole. A recent article by Renato Lattes dedicated to Turin gives us a splendid summary of what the system meant in terms of daily economic democracy:

> The period between 1971 and 1977 was probably the high point of workers' contractual power, given the delegates' constant capacity at that time to negotiate shop-floor conditions. This was certainly the case for FIAT, and was probably so for the greater part of the Turin factories boasting high levels of trade unionism. The delegates intervened on a vast range of issues: work rhythms, manning levels, pauses, production-line speeds; environmental improvements, health and safety dangers at

work, exposure to noxious substances, information on high-risk practices in the factories; levels of skill (*qualifiche*) and the rotation and reorganisation of functions; negotiation of shift work and the reduction of night shifts; the introduction of freshly prepared food in the canteen, etc. The protagonists of all this activity were delegates of considerable experience, who had political or trade union training, and sometimes technical and scientific skills deriving from paid study leave (the 150-Hours Scheme, which had been incorporated into the national engineering contract of 1973). They were also accustomed to long and complex negotiations in the factories, and were often leaders who had emerged or been selected during the very many factory and shop meetings of the time, or else during the negotiations themselves.[18]

Here is a vision, fleeting but detailed, of what participation might come to mean at the workplace. In Millian terms, it leads to the formation of skilled and cultured representatives of the working classes, constantly present and active in the workplace, deliberating on the basis of parity with employers. In Marxist terms, there are here present the first, significant steps to overcoming alienation and to reclaiming control over the production process, although not yet over the commodities being produced.

The second example is Rudolf Meidner's scheme for collective investment funds, again of the 1970s. Meidner and Gosta Rehn had been the co-architects of Sweden's post-war welfare state. Each year, according to Meidner's scheme, every large Swedish corporation was to be required to issue to its employees shares equivalent to 20 per cent of its profits. These shares were not to be owned individually but were to be entrusted to regional management boards. The boards were to be made democratically accountable, and they were to use the income from the shares to promote social priorities and the public interest. The shares could not be transferred. As the community's stake in the large enterprises grew, so too would its ability to influence corporate decision-making. Meidner's scheme attracted a great deal of attention, but was never put into practice. This was partly because of the Swedish employers' intransigent hostility to any threat to ownership rights and partly because by the end of the 1970s that great wave of participatory energy to which I made earlier reference had ebbed away.[19]

In 1977 a book was published in Milan on participation and industrial democracy. It called for 'industrial democracy' to be realised in three areas: in the social structure surrounding the workplace, in the structure of firms themselves, and in the productive process. There was nothing special about these proposals, except that the authors were not trade unionists or left-wing politicians but representatives of the Italian young industrial entrepreneurs' association.[20] We have gone a long way backwards since then.

I want to end this discussion by returning for a moment to the European Union. In the last few years the Union has issued important regulations and directives regarding the participation of workers in firms which wish to qualify for the appellation 'European business' or 'European cooperative business'. The registration of these firms, which harbour the ambition of expanding freely their activities in an ever-growing European market, has been made subordinate to their recognising workers' rights to information, consultation and participation. This is a significant step forward, to be compared to the directives on participation which the Union has issued in other fields. It is a small but significant sign that the theme of economic democracy is not entirely moribund.

However, the same caveats and discriminations that we

used in the field of political democracy must also be applied here. How far are these directives mere window dressing and how far are they really the beginnings of an ongoing process of involvement of workers and their representatives in democratic decision-making? Expert trade-union opinion is not very hopeful.[21] One trade union commentator notes that the norms regarding workers' participation are 'pervaded by an intimate contradiction': they were conceived in the 1970s, re-elaborated laboriously in the 1980s and 1990s, and finally came into being in an economic climate so radically different from thirty years earlier that participation was no longer really on the agenda.[22] Another regrets that 'a good part of these years has been lost in interminable controversies . . . The regulations' texts bear the imprint of this protracted labour. On the one hand they have become excessively complex, on the other they lack transparency and legibility.'[23] Once again, we find the Union paralysed by a lack of overall political vision. It is a point I would like to return to at the end of this book.

## 2

## DEMOCRACY AND GENDER

Time and fashion play many tricks. Until a few years ago John
Stuart Mill was best remembered for *On Liberty*, while the
work he published in 1869, *The Subjection of Women*, was very
largely ignored. As evidence of this affirmation it is sufficient
to note that Paul Smart, in his in many ways insightful 1991
comparison *Mill and Marx*, a work which bears the subtitle
*Individual Liberty and the Roads to Freedom*, does not discuss
Mill's views on female emancipation at all.[24] Nowadays, *The
Subjection of Women* is one of the most translated, discussed
and studied of all Mill's texts.

Behind this renewed interest lies the pressing question of
the relationship between gender and democracy. The reinvention and, one might say, the reanimation of democracy are
intimately connected to it. Although the definition of what has
come to be known as 'gender' is a complex and controversial
matter, it can be taken here to be the reality and representation
of difference, set within the historical context of male domi-
nance. Gender permeates both the political and economic
spheres, and in many ways determines their particular forms
and configurations. To have a clear idea of the present state of
gender relations within democracy, and to see how they could
and should be changed, is as important as seeking new political forms which combine representative and participative
democracy, or trying to create a system of economic democracy. Yet all too often the question is relegated into a ghetto of
women's studies, or treated very summarily.

Mill's principal intent in his now famous text is, as usual, stated at its outset with great force and clarity. He wishes to argue that

> the principle which regulates the existing social relations between the two sexes – the legal subordination of one sex to the other – is wrong in itself, and now one of the chief hindrances to human improvement; and that it ought to be replaced by a principle of perfect equality, admitting no power or privilege on the one side, nor disability on the other.[25]

The first of Mill's concerns, then, is the abolition of women's legal subordination to men. This has largely been achieved in Western democracies, though often only very recently.[26] His second concern, though, the creation of 'a principle of perfect equality', remains very distant as an objective.

Mill conducts his argument for the achievement of equality on a number of different levels. One of the most important is that in which he contests the male representation of the unchanging and unchangeable *nature of women* as meek, submissive and yielding to the control of others. This, argues Mill, is what men desire and what they have trained women to become, but 'what is now called the nature of women is an eminently artificial thing – the result of forced repression in some directions, unnatural stimulation in others'.[27] His, too, is the refusal to accept that the private and the public spheres correspond symmetrically and automatically to the innate characteristics of the two sexes, with women necessarily confined to the first of these spheres. Mill is convinced rather that the liberation of women will bring great benefits to the public sphere, adding greatly 'to the amount of individual talent available for the conduct of human affairs, which are certainly not at present so abundantly provided in that respect that they can afford to dispense with one-half of what nature offers'.[28]

However, when it comes to the propositional part of Mill's reflections, on how in practice to 'admit no power or privilege' for one sex at the expense of the other, his remedies are rather limited. He considers the single greatest weapon in this battle to be the franchise, but obviously he wishes to apply to women the same distinctions and limitations as he does to men. His other propositions are the reform of the gross inequalities of the British marriage law of the time, and the creation of greater opportunities for female education and employment. They seem all too limited to modern eyes, but we must place them in the context of Mill's long campaign against Victorian conformism, 'that mass of feelings to be contended against', as he called them, 'which gather round and protect old institutions and customs'.[29]

Furthermore, Mill was convinced that it was not up to him to lay down a programme for female emancipation. Once women were accorded equal rights, it would be for they themselves to explore the contours of their own ambitions and desires in the political sphere, as elsewhere. Such a position corresponded totally to his view of individual autonomy, whether male or female, and individual self-improvement and self-discipline. Once women were indistinguishable from men as individuals, with the same education and rights, then 'perfect equality' would be achieved. Mill embraced this vision, seeing in it an enormous benefit not only for women but for mankind as a whole.[30]

How earnestly Mill held these views can be gauged from an extraordinary formal letter he wrote in March, 1851, on the occasion of his marriage to Harriet Taylor. In it he renounced all the privileges which British marriage laws conveyed upon him:

I, having no means of legally divesting myself of these odious powers ... declare it to be my will and intention, and the condition of the engagement between us, that she retains in all respects whatever the same absolute freedom of action, and freedom of disposal of herself and of all that does or may at any time belong to her, as if no such marriage had taken place; and I absolutely disclaim and repudiate all pretension to have acquired any *rights* whatever by virtue of such marriage.[31]

*The Subjection of Women*, though, contains at least one passage in which its author shows himself to be heavily influenced by that very conformism which he himself had done so much to denounce. Without establishing a rigidly gendered private–public divide, Mill none the less assumes that it is the man's principal function to earn a livelihood and the woman's to take responsibility for home and family:

Like a man when he chooses a profession, so, when a woman marries, it may in general be understood that she makes the choice of the management of a household, and the bringing up of a family, as the first call upon her exertions, during as many years of her life as may be required for the purpose; and that she renounces, not all other objects and occupations, but all of which are not consistent with the requirements of this.[32]

As for Marx, his reflections on the condition of women were much more limited. *Capital* and his other economic works are full of passionate, detailed and indignant denunciations of the inhuman conditions of women and children workers in the factories of his time. The 'Communist Manifesto' contains a famous passage on the hypocrisies of the bourgeois family, on how women were little more than chattels, and how men's frequent adultery transformed bourgeois marriage into 'a system of wives in common'.[33] Where Mill chose to reason against prevailing public opinion, Marx wanted to shock it to its core. He succeeded magnificently, if not in the short term, because his works were little known and read in his own lifetime, then certainly in the long run. But on the specific question that interests us here, the connection between gender and democracy, he has next to nothing to say. His view on this, as on other matters which belonged to the 'superstructure', was that all would change with revolution and the abolition of the capitalist system of production. In other words, he gives us no idea of how the democratic public sphere would be different once women's emancipation had been achieved.

~

Turning now to the modern world, I would like first to consider the question of gender *equality* in the public sphere, before turning to the crucial but controversial question of *difference* in the same sphere. On this latter subject it would be fair to say that neither Mill nor Marx had anything much to offer.

Educational equality – one of the fields closest to Mill's heart – has taken great strides in many modern democracies. In the field of tertiary education, for instance, over the last thirty years there has been an almost vertical rise in the enrolment of women in Latin American universities, while in most countries in the OECD, though not in Switzerland, not only are there more women than men at university, but their academic performance is superior.[34]

Progress is much more muted in other fields. Women are systematically penalised in labour markets all over the world, and their wages and salaries are nowhere equal to those of men for the same work performed. In very many democracies, female representation in public institutions remains woefully sparse, in spite of women often having obtained suffrage more than fifty years ago. The franchise is clearly not the all-powerful instrument which Mill hoped it would be. By and large, women's votes are not translated into women's presence in politics, and women's professional capabilities do not succeed in penetrating the higher ranks of public administration. In a recent study of senior civil servants in Japan, just three of the 502 subjects were women.[35] In Italy a woefully low number of women have become Members of Parliament, presidents of regions, senior civil servants and so on. As is well known, the four Scandinavian countries, Sweden, Finland, Norway and Denmark, have the best record in this respect and consistently head the gender parity tables of the United Nations Development Programme.[36] However, even in the cold and civilised North the number of women MPs and cabinet ministers only reaches one-third of the total, while the OECD average is under one-sixth.[37]

Nor is it at all safe to claim that Western democracies are the most attentive to the question of gender parity in the political sphere. It was India, not Britain or the United States, that in 1993 took the dramatically necessary but much contested step of legislating that an obligatory minimum of 33 per cent of councillors in local governments (*panchayats*) must be women, thus revolutionising representation at a local level. Even here, the resistance of male politicians was ferocious.[38]

Laura Balbo, a sociologist who was for a time Italy's minister for equal opportunities, offers an overall summary of the problem which has more than Italian relevance: 'I collect statistics and perceive mechanisms which testify to the permanent asymmetry, inequality and discrimination existing between men and women, in the world of politics in particular. And I realise that this asymmetry is energetic, effective, and of great weight.'[39] Why do these stubborn impediments to gender equality in modern democracies continue to exist? There are at least two possible answers, one lying within the political sphere and one outside it.

The first is that the political systems of modern democracies, as they came to be formed in the twentieth century, are male organisations reflecting primarily male values, culture and traditions. In this sense they are highly *gendered*. Nowadays there is hardly a male democratic politician who does not pay lip service to the need for gender equality in the political sphere. But when the cards are down, and a choice of personnel has to be made at local, regional or national level, then men invariably choose other men. To quote Balbo again: 'A logic is at work in political institutions which ensures the reproduction of the existing; it functions by guaranteeing the conditions which produce exclusion or retard the inclusion of *those who remain on the outside*: women, obviously, but also members of other minorities.'[40] Guaranteed quotas for women, as in India's panchayats, are in operation at different levels in some other democracies, too.[41] But quotas do not touch the deeper culture of these political systems, which are by their very nature exclusive rather than inclusive, steeped in traditions and practices which only men have created. Parliaments have always been men's clubs. Today they are men's clubs that admit women.

The second explanation of the asymmetries noted by Balbo lies outside the political sphere. It takes us back to what I wrote in Part II about the need to create a much stronger system of connections between families, civil society and the state. Individual women, especially those who occupy the central (and often maternal) role in what have become extended three-generational families, and who work outside the home as well, may now be the legal equals of their partners, but have great difficulty in finding the time, energy and emotional liberty to dedicate even part of their lives to the public sphere. For all their expertise in negotiating the complexities of everyday existence, there is a limit to what they can undertake.

Certainly gender imbalances within the family have lessened in the last thirty years, but it would be a conceit to suggest that they have disappeared. Home life, like political life, continues to be gendered in a particular and largely traditional way. And democratic states do little or nothing to ease the path of women into public life, either at local or national level. The problem of participation is left to chance and circumstance. Never is it tackled at its roots.

Time and again in my experience of civil society, even in families with a heightened sense of gender justice, it is wives and mothers who send their men to meetings and choose, or are obliged, to stay at home to look after children or ageing parents, or to fulfil domestic duties. If we think about the possible connections between individual life cycles and active presence in civil society, then we see immediately that the women who are most committed are either those who are pre- or post-child rearing, or those who have consciously chosen to limit their family obligations in one way or another. And to enter politics, with its frenetic, time-consuming, evening-oriented rhythms, obviously all of male origin, is even more difficult. To do so, women have simply to become like men.

~

Let us, though, suppose for a moment that Mill's 'perfect equality' has been realised, and that women are as numerically present as men at all levels of democracy. There still remains the crucial question of gender *difference*. Franca Bimbi and Alisa Del Re have written in this regard:

> It is worth asking if the inclusion of women in a sphere of citizenship moulded in origin by men has been sufficient to produce an adequate model of citizenship for the female sex. Perhaps it would be more correct to say that women's effective inclusion should not *ab origine* have taken place without democracy and its rules having been totally refounded.[42]

When discussing gender difference, it is important to *invert* its habitual ordering, which over the centuries has taken for granted the 'natural' superiority of men and the equally natural submission of women. Millicent Fawcett noted at the beginning of the twentieth century that women could be adequately represented by men so long as the two sexes resembled each other completely, but, since they did not, women's difference found no expression in the political system of the time.[43] A century later Mrs Fawcett's point is still largely valid. The adequate expression of difference in the public sphere is not just ensured by the franchise and by an equal numerical presence of women and men. It is, rather, a question of culture, of a different way of setting agendas, choosing priorities and conducting business; of institutions and administrations behaving in a different way through being gendered in a different way.

Of course it would be foolish and mistaken to claim that women's behaviour, in contrast to that of men, incarnates every virtue and natural superiority. In a recent discussion of the BBC global project *Why Democracy?*, a series of ten films broadcast in October 2007 to some 200 countries, one of the key questions asked was: 'Are women more democratic?' The general answer seemed to be a resounding 'no'. One of the most eloquent of these rejections came from the American writer Katie Roiphe:

> In certain circles, liberal-minded ladies still muse wistfully on how much better the world would be, how much more peaceful, how many fewer wars, how much less political ugliness, if only women ruled it! This perspective seems to me to involve either crass dishonesty or complete amnesia from anyone who has ever been a little girl. Has anyone on earth ever been nastier, more brutal, than little girls? . . . The hierarchies between women are so rigid, so patrolled, so absolute, it seems ludicrous to pretend that women in power would be more democratic, more inclusive, more generous to those who are less fortunate . . .[44]

None the less, this is only one side of the argument. Female difference and specificity, as the American political philosopher Martha Nussbaum has argued, do emerge constantly in a distinctive and recommendable form: both with regard to certain moral *virtues* such as caring, peacefulness, patience, inclusiveness, attention to intimate and everyday relations and needs; and to certain moral *abilities*, such as that of perceiving intuitively the needs of others and being able to respond resourcefully to those needs.[45] The conscious transposition of such values, which some may wish to regard as universal but which are very often expressed in the modern world by female voices, would revolutionise democratic practices and agendas. And if care became the ethical basis of citizenship? Our parliaments, guided by such ideas, would be very different places.

# 3

## TIME AND SCALE

There are obvious difficulties with, and objections to, the sort of reanimated and repopulated democracy for which I have been arguing in this book. It is a particularly demanding sort of democracy which refuses to confine politics to a separate and distant professional sphere, which tries instead to combine representation with participation, which contests the condition whereby individuals are citizens in the political sphere but mere subordinates at work, and which demands a public sphere whose workings and priorities are gendered in a radically different way. But no less than this, I would argue, is now necessary to resuscitate and protect democracy as we know it. The most serious objections to such a vision have to do with time and scale. Let me deal with them in turn.

### Time

The question of time in a society which is not time-rich but time-poor, and which is dominated by work-and-spend routines, is a very serious one. How are people to find time, in a society like ours, for the sort of democracy I have sketched out in the pages above? There are various levels at which to address this question. The first concerns individuals. As I underlined earlier in this essay, and as I hope has become abundantly clear, I do not have in mind a form of Jacobin democracy, where participation becomes a daily obligation. Participation is voluntary, to be encouraged and nurtured, not

enforced. Not all individuals will, or can, be active in a democratic public sphere during the whole course of their lives. If
we study individual life cycles, then we see there are dips and
peaks, moments of intimate withdrawal and others of greater
openness. It is not that individuals have no time, but that they
are not *accustomed* to making time for the public sphere. Mill
hits the nail on the head: 'So true is it that unnatural generally
means only uncustomary, and that everything which is usual
appears natural.'[46]

Putting aside a few hours every week for matters of public
interest could quite easily come to seem customary, especially if those who now hold political power in democracies
thought such an objective worthy of encouragement. Under
the honeyed routines of consumer capitalism, to pass a great
many hours in hypermarkets and shopping centres has now
become quite 'natural'. *A priori* there is nothing to prevent
time spent in improving democracy from becoming a habitual
part of people's lives. Such a prospect does not offer material
rewards, but quite possibly a greater meaning to life – something which is often deeply felt as lacking today.

~

A second level of reply lies with the ever growing possibilities
of modern information technology to save time and facilitate
deliberation. The amount of information that can be garnered
from the world wide web, the rapidity of communication, the
popularity of blogs, open publishing/editing systems, webcast-
ing and podcasting, the way meetings and mobilisations can be
organised by e-mail, even the possibility of decision-making
by computer voting – these have all become commonplaces
when listing the democratic advantages of the information-

technology revolution. Internet access, like television before it, is spreading with great rapidity. In April–June 2001 just over a third of British households had it; by the end of 2006 this figure had doubled.[47] Although clearly slanted in class and educational terms, broadband access is also increasing very rapidly. One has only to visit a high-quality website and discussion forum like openDemocracy.net to realise the potential of the web.

However, the advantages should not be exaggerated, nor the dangers ignored. These latter can be analysed under three headings: control, time and quality. Over the last two decades corporate control of the internet has increased ominously. By 2001 four internet service providers controlled half of all user minutes of US citizens, AOL-Time Warner alone controlling almost a third. In 2005 Rupert Murdoch's giant News Corps media corporation bought the social networking site MySpace for $580 million.[48] In the competition for viewers' attention, the large corporations boast huge marketing and advertising advantages. Here, too, there is little that resembles a level playing field.

Second, the question of time. One of the most fascinating paradoxes of contemporary life is that the internet both saves and consumes our time. Communications between persons and associations are extraordinarily accelerated, but at the same time much more frequent. 'Doing your e-mails' has become a major occupation and time consumer for professionals. Couples often sit at home for hours staring into a screen, while their children's time is eaten away by games that have become addictions.

Third, the question of quality. The quality of information on the internet is highly variable, and a great deal of time can be wasted sorting the wheat from the chaff. In civil society e-mail discussions can often become brittle and interminable, with those who have the most time and are the most long-winded writing the most. All those who study civil society concur that correspondence is a poor substitute for face-to-face meetings.[49]

We should not, in other words, make the same mistake that Mill made with the railways – the real transformative element lies not with the technology itself but the use we make of it. The internet, however innovative, is not intrinsically democratic. Its use embraces many contested areas – access and connectivity, protocol, network regulation, intellectual property and electronic surveillance. None the less, it can be a very precious enabling tool, if we allow for its ambivalences and dangers. It can help us to save time, be better informed and be in closer and more frequent contact one with another. And its possibilities are only just beginning to be realised.[50]

~

A third level of reply lies with the nature of deliberation itself. If deliberative democracy – in civil society, in a workplace council or in the local state – is left in a chaotic and primitive form, then a great deal of time will be wasted and the popularity of the form will soon be dissipated. Instead, the sort of democracy that I have in mind needs strict deadlines, clear objectives and a great deal of Millian self-discipline on the part of all involved. This is not a culture of participation that will be learned overnight. But if a reformed (dare I say repentant?) political class is convinced of its value, then it will invest resources – in terms of publicity, facilitators, coordinators, meeting places etc. – which will speed the process on its way.

These are some possible answers to the question *How*

*will people make the time for democracy of this sort?* A second
and connected question, institutional rather than individual,
also deserves to be posed and answered: *Will democracy be
swamped by excessive participation, to the extent that it will
become unworkable?* Samuel Huntington feared something
of this sort, when he wrote in the early 1980s of the danger of
'overloaded government'.[51] Certainly, at first sight the presence
of more political subjects, in more areas of life, involved in
more deliberative arenas, seems to carry with it the prospect of
decision-making being impossibly protracted and subject to
endless compromise. The risk of paralysis is clear for all to see.

Here the example of Porto Alegre comes to our aid. The
idea of an annual cycle of participation and decision-making, accompanied at the beginning of each year by a rigorous
assessment of results achieved in the previous one, is a precious
indication of how participation and efficiency can potentially
proceed hand-in-hand. Once again the *tightness* of the deliberative process is all-important. So, too, is the administrative
culture of the city, region or nation in question. If administrative procedures are slow and complicated, then democratic
government, whether elitist or participatory, will be faced with
the same difficulties. The administrative culture of Brazil leaves
a lot to be desired, and the results in Porto Alegre have been
far from perfect. But deliberation brings such administrative
inadequacies out into the open, where previously problems
were resolved undemocratically, if at all, through clientelist
networks and corporate lobbying..

There is a final consideration worth airing. It has a counterfactual air to it, and refers to what happens if forms of popular
involvement in decision-making are not adopted. Small and
separate groups of decision-makers, isolated from societal
realities, often make poor decisions. The case of the Val di Susa

in north-western Italy, and that of Antonio Gaudi's Sagrada Familia in Barcelona, both involve plans imposed from above for the construction of high-speed train lines and tunnels. In the first case a whole alpine community organised against the plans, with some 30,000 people bringing the works to a complete standstill. In the second the proposal to construct a tunnel for the high-speed AVE line so close to the cathedral, with the attendant risk of undermining its foundations, has been widely denounced both in Barcelona and elsewhere. In modern societies, decisions taken with no popular involvement can easily lead to a greater degree of paralysis than those which are the result of a consciously controlled process of participative democracy.

## *Scale*

As for scale, we return to the fundamental objection raised by Constant and by Mill. The direct, physical presence of citizens can only be assured in small communities, while in modern complex societies democratic government must perforce be indirect and representative. Even if the combined form of democracy – representative and participative – can be shown to have worked in a big city like Porto Alegre over an extended period of time, can this experience have more than a local significance and dimension? This is an important question and we should keep an open mind about it. But it is worth noting that even if the model were functional only on a local level, it would still be a great step forward in terms of the reinvigoration of municipal democracy.

I think we can go further, cautiously. Although many politicians and academics deny the possibility of transnational politics on any but an elite basis, there is a growing literature about forms of democratic accountability on a global level, and the possibilities of creating a 'cosmopolitan' democracy.[52] In response to the great tide of neo-liberal globalisation which has concentrated major choices in the hands of very restricted economic and political elites, a large number of counter-measures have been proposed, though none has yet progressed further than the drawing board. Continental referenda, the democratic strengthening and reform of the ONU, global regional parliaments (such as for Latin America), a transnational Court of Human Justice with jurisdiction over all states, even a World Parliament, have been among the proposals. Although all these have to do with democratisation, and many of them are urgent priorities for world politics, few of them are concerned with participatory politics of the sort I have been describing. Indeed, at first sight it is difficult to imagine how they could be. The larger the scale, the blunter the democratic instrument at our disposal.

However, this general rule needs to be qualified, at least in part. New forms of participation are being invented to meet this most severe of challenges. They are always more limited than the face-to-face deliberation and decision-making possible in a local setting, but they are far from negligible. Let me take the example of a continental or global region referendum. This would be a very valuable mechanism on issues such as global warming or international trade agreements. If any such referendum were to take place in the future, it could benefit greatly from the proposals put forward recently by James Fishkin and Bruce Ackerman for what they call 'a deliberation day'.[53] Their scheme was designed for an American context and more specifically for the presidential elections, but it could certainly have wider applications.

Basically, what they propose is that after a first television debate between presidential candidates, there is a ten-day pause, after which a new public holiday, to be called 'Deliberation Day' is declared. Differently from 'Thanksgiving Day', it is not dedicated to rejoicing and family reunions, but to forms of structured debate at various levels, especially local, about the relative merits of the two presidential candidates. Put simply, *time is made* for the nation to take seriously deliberation and choice. And after the new national holiday, there is a further phase of discussion at various levels, prior to the national vote. Of course, many Americans may well choose to sleep late that day, or have a trip out instead of taking part in discussions. But the challenge of Ackerman and Fishkin is very much that of Mill – to make customary and habitual what at first looks strange and unnatural. And this same challenge and methodology could well be applied, with all the support that e-democracy could offer, to transnational experiments like continental referenda.

~

I would like to consider one other aspect of participatory transnational politics. This time it is not a mechanism (like Deliberation Day) but a social movement. Over the past decade, as I mentioned earlier, there has been an extraordinary growth of global civil society. This movement has taken very many forms, one of the most significant of which has been the unstable, frequently chaotic but exhilarating experience of social forums at local, continental and global levels. The World Social Forums have played an invaluable role in creating a diffuse, alternative culture to neo-liberalism, as well as stimulating the growth of a huge variety of research, campaigns and international networks.

Side-by-side with this movement, and receiving an enormous input from it, INGOS (international non-governmental organisations) have greatly increased their presence and strength in the public sphere of international governance.[54]

How does this translate, if at all, into transnational participatory *democracy*? There are obvious shortcomings, pitfalls, and dangers which should not simply be swept under the carpet. Here is a short list of some of them: NGOs may well not be democratic organisations themselves, or else in the hands of small groups of professional activists. Some NGOs may not be genuine at all, but rather, as I mentioned earlier, GONGOS – government operated non-governmental organisations, invented in order to mask human-rights violations by dictatorial governments. Some Northern INGOS speak for Southern, developing countries, but do so in terms of patronising benevolence. Informality and spontaneity are essential to social movements, but democracy has need of structure and clear rules. Finally, it is not ever entirely clear what *demos* Social Forums or INGOS actually represent, in whose name, apart from their own, they purport to speak.

None the less, global civil society has an invaluable role to play at the level of a transnational public sphere. This is not the *same* role, structured and direct, of the participatory budget at Porto Alegre, nor could it be. It has to do, rather, with the creation of alternative global voices, with the opening up of previously secretive and non-accountable spheres, with the diffusion on a mass scale of relevant information and documentation, and with increasing the number of relevant actors, or stakeholders, present when crucial international decisions are taken. For no one is this more important than weaker or less privileged global actors such as those who represent developing countries or their often fragile NGOs.

In the last fifteen years transnational civil society has begun to interact with nearly all international organisations, though its capacity to influence outcomes varies widely. Let me take just two examples, one quite well known, the other less so. Formally speaking, the World Trade Organisation (WTO) operates on the basis of equal voting rights for all nation-states. In reality it retains important elements of the 'club model' of international cooperation, based upon decisions being taken by the few and the powerful. The famous 'green room' consultations at ministerial conferences of the WTO (usually confined to between just ten and twenty-five member states) have become synonymous for what has been rightly called the 'obscure and secretive ways of international decision making'.[55] No minutes of these meetings were ever taken. The contesting of the 'club model' by INGOs and the World Social Forums has had an enormous effect in terms of accountability, of making available to a wider public the information upon which decisions were taken and in widening the number of stakeholders who play an effective part in decision-making in the crucial area of world trade.

The second example is more a micro- than a macro- one, but comes from an equally crucial area, that of human rights. Recently the United Nations High Commission for Human Rights was transformed into a Human Rights Council. Opinions differ sharply about the value of this move, though the UN points to the fact that there will be more resources available, that the Council is properly elected from among the nations of the UN and that it will meet three times a year, whereas it previously met only once. At the initial meeting of the Council in June 2006 the space reserved for the intervention of any but nation-states' representatives was very limited. However, some sixty NGOs got together to contest this decision. Instead

of demanding to speak themselves, they chose four distin-
guished voices, three female and one male, to ensure that the
global viewpoint of the human-rights NGOs was heard. The
speakers were Arnold Tsunga from Zimbabwe, Natasa Kandic
from Serbia, Sunila Abeysekera from Sri Lanka and Marta
Vazquez from Argentina. Vazquez's speech closed the session
in a memorable and moving way:

> I am still asking myself why I am here before you today . . .
> And that question has brought me to reflect on the last
> thirty years of my family life, overshadowed during the
> Argentine Military Dictatorship [of 1976–83] by the abduction
> and enforced disappearance of my daughter, Maria Marta,
> together with her husband Cesar, an event which took place on
> that evil night of 14 May 1976 . . .
> In May 1977 I joined the fledgling movement of the Mothers
> of Plaza de Mayo, then sarcastically called the 'Mad Women'
> by the authorities. Together with those fellow women I began a
> learning process . . . Currently I am President of the Mothers of
> Plaza de Mayo (Founders Line) Association . . .
> Impunity has been the hallmark characteristic of the
> practice of enforced disappearances. And that is why NGOs
> require the full application of justice in every country affected. It
> is why we are concerned about the way the international law for
> the protection of human rights is exercised and respected, and
> about the creation of legal mechanisms which set out sanctions
> and impede the perpetrations of this crime against humanity. I
> want to share with you the great importance which families and
> NGOs attach to an International Convention against Enforced
> Disappearances [later approved by the Council] . . .
> In all my long endeavours I, together with my companions,
> have always been against all violence and have never asked
> for vengeance . . . I hope to continue always in the struggle for
> Memory, Truth and Justice.[56]

This second example is above all a symbolic one, but no

less relevant for that. It has to do with the one of the under-lying questions of the whole of this book: *Which voices will be heard, to what effect, in which arenas?* The arena of inter-national governance is populated by the voices of diplomats, politicians, bureaucrats and functional specialists. Its proce-dures are opaque and it is far from citizens. But it is not an impregnable or impenetrable sphere.

# 4

## BACK TO THE EUROPEAN UNION

The above discussion has more than passing relevance for the European Union. We left the Union at an earlier stage of this book as a 'sleeping giant', its own democracy built largely on sand and subject to growing popular disaffection, a giant unable to invent a democracy of its own. This impression is confirmed if we examine the relevant sections of the Rome Treaty of 2004 establishing a Constitution for Europe. The Constitution, as we have seen, was abandoned after the French and Dutch electorates voted against its ratification. None the less it offers an interesting insight into the way the European elites view the question of representation and participation within the Union. It can safely be said that, far from being an answer to transnational disaffection, the Constitution was timid in the extreme. It represents another vital opportunity missed.

The relevant section (Part I, Title VI) of the Constitution was entitled, rather hopefully in view of past performance 'The democratic life of the Union'. Article I-46, paragraph 1, stated unequivocally that the Union's functioning is founded on the principle of representative democracy. Article I-47 was, instead, dedicated to the principle of participative democracy, which at first sight certainly appears an encouraging and innovative sign. However, it soon becomes clear that the Union's activity is in no way *founded* upon participation, and that there is a clear hierarchy of importance and indeed separation between the two principles – representative and participatory. In linguistic terms it is revealing to analyse certain key phrases of article I-47, for they betray the intent to keep participation firmly in the field of consultation and discussion. Thus, the institutions of the Union 'shall, by appropriate means, give citizens and representative associations the opportunity *to make known and publicly exchange* their views in all areas of Union action' (paragraph 1). The same institutions 'shall *maintain an open, transparent and regular dialogue* with representative associations and civil society' (paragraph 2). The Commission promises '*broad consultations* with parties concerned in order to ensure that the Union's actions are coherent and transparent' (paragraph 3). The italics are mine.[57]

In this text there is no combining or intertwining of the two forms of democracy. The one is sovereign, the other, once again, subsidiary or auxiliary. As for gender and democracy, article II-83 establishes parity between the sexes and specifically notes, obviously with quotas in mind, that the principle of equality 'shall not prevent the maintenance or adoption of measures providing for specific advantages in favour of the under-represented sex'.[58] But there is not even a whisper to suggest that gender *difference*, with its promise of the reordering of the agendas of the political sphere, might merit a mention in the constitution of Europe.

Furthermore, the Constitution proposed a popular, but highly indirect way of ensuring the actuation of parts of the Constitution. An 'initiative' signed by at least a million citizens from a 'relevant number' of states can invite the Commission to present an appropriate proposal. This is much less than a European referendum, and little more than a petition. It has been widely criticised for its limited nature. Small wonder that the Constitution aroused so little initial enthusiasm.

Worse was to come. Instead of responding to the widespread criticism of the Treaty for its insufficiency in the field of democracy, those who were responsible for preparing its successor, the Treaty of Lisbon, which was signed in December 2007, went backwards rather than forwards. The principle of participatory democracy which, however vaguely, had been enshrined in Article I-47 of the Constitution, has disappeared in the new treaty. In the new version only the 'initiative' signed by more than a million citizens, *inviting* the Commission to consider an appropriate proposal, remains as a token to participatory democracy.

The drafters of the ill-fated European Constitution placed a quotation from Thucydides at its very beginning: 'Our Constitution bears the name of democracy because power is not in the hands of the few but of the many'. Unfortunately, exactly the opposite continues to be true of the Union.

Yet the potential of the Union remains great. For many countries it has had an invaluable regulatory role, leading nation-states along paths – such as that of equal opportunities – which they would not naturally have followed. And we have seen how the Union, even if sometimes with exasperating slowness, has issued important criteria, regulations and directives on such key issues for democracy as workers' participation in new European businesses.[59] A whole panoply of rights has been enunciated and often enforced by the European Court of Justice. Many believe, with justification, that the European legal order is far ahead of its polity. What is needed, therefore, is some sort of quantum leap in democratic thinking, a new ability to link European citizens effectively to their institutions. Without that rethinking, disaffection and torpor can only continue.

One approach to this problem, that of Michael Newman and others, is to stress that there can be no progress in the EU without democracy being first revitalised at a local level.[60] It is difficult to disagree with him, and indeed much of this book has intentionally been concerned with the micro-politics of democracy. However, there is nothing to prevent this bottom-up approach being accompanied, and indeed encouraged, by initiatives from above. In theoretical terms, this would certainly imply the abandonment of the vague and unsatisfactory principle of subsidiarity, which has borne such meagre democratic fruits in the last twenty years.

What is needed instead is for the Union to embrace a *theory of combined democracy* which intertwines in a meaningful way representation and participation. It could then start inventing ways of translating that theory into reality, transforming itself into the facilitator and promoter of a highly original project. Facilitation in this context would mean research, experiments in combined democracy in different parts of the Union, and investment in information and other resources which would enable citizens to experience different forms of self-government.[61] The 'sleeping giant' could stir and partially reinvent itself. Its immense resources could then at last be directed in some small part towards encouraging the creation of virtuous circles of democratic participation, instead of ever-greater distancing in a decaying model of representative democracy.

# EPILOGUE

## MARX AND MILL IN HEAVEN, SPRING 2008

*A cloud somewhere over Europe. The top of the cloud has been flattened out as if to form a stage.*

*Enter* John Stuart Mill, *stage right. He is wearing walking shoes, and has just been on a long botanical expedition with his friend, the entomologist Jean Henri Fabre.*

*Enter* Karl Marx, *stage left. He has recently been promoted from Purgatory, and is finally cured of his carbuncles. He carries a book, which he is annotating furiously.*

*Both men are equipped with powerful telescopes, from which they view the progress of the world.*

~

MILL (*looking up from his telescope*): My dear Karl – that is if I may use your first name after all these years – how pleased I am to see you in such good form!

MARX: Let us waste no time before taking up again our discussion where we were constrained to leave it in 1873. It seems to me, John Stuart – if that is the right way to address you – that, economically speaking, we were both in the right and both in the wrong. I must first admit that I mistook the birth of capitalism for its death pangs. The rate of profit [*coughs apologetically*] does not fall. The workers do not rise up, ever stronger; they do not organise themselves as a revolutionary class. They seem to be – how shall I put it – ah yes, more interested in appropriation than expropriation!! Down there [*nods derisively towards the earth*], they talk about late capitalism, late modernity, late everything. But how do they know what time it is, economically speaking? How do they know if it is late or early? [*He pauses and continues in a softer tone.*] But I hope you will not deny that I foresaw many things in the capitalism of today, not least its ever greater concentration and rapaciousness on a global scale.

MILL: Now that I have had abundant time to read all your works, my dear Karl, I can confirm, without a shadow of doubt, that you have been capitalism's greatest analyst. As for myself, there is little to say. I greatly mistook [*coughs apologetically*] the virtuous consequences of competition, and I overestimated the self-righting capacities of the market. What has occurred recently on a global scale, and all in the name of liberalism, fills me with abhorrence. It is not thus that we can hope to create a peaceful and prosperous world order. Individuals seem to have lost all sense of material modesty and collective responsibility . . . [*He breaks off and takes up his telescope again*] But what is this I see? [*Chuckles*]. We are the subject of comparison.

*Marx looks worried.*

MILL (*adjusting the focus of the telescope*): Here we are. Good gracious – we find ourselves in unlikely company. The pamphlet, very richly illustrated if I may say so, is called 'A true Italian story'. It is a piece of electoral propaganda, full of photographs of Silvio Berlusconi. Perhaps you have been following his career – he is the Italian business man and politician who compares himself to Napoleon.

MARX: So does Sarkozy.

MILL: Yes indeed. Now what does Berlusconi have to say about us? It is but a small insert, accompanied by both our portraits. [*He reads, and his face clouds over.*] I am afraid I am the hero once again. But on what basis? My good God! Listen to the opinions I am supposed to hold: 'Between individualism and socialism it is necessary to choose the first, which guarantees individual liberty without impeding the struggle against social injustice.' But do they not know that the last words ever printed of mine are the following: 'Society is fully entitled to abrogate or alter any particular right of property which on sufficient consideration it judges to stand in the way of the public good. And assuredly the terrible case which, as we saw in a former chapter, Socialists are able to make out against the present economic order of society, demands a full consideration of all means by which the institution may have a chance of being made to work in a manner more beneficial to that large portion of society which at present enjoys the least share of its direct benefits.'

MARX: Your memory, John Stuart . . .

MILL: I am simply called by my first name, John . . .

MARX: . . . seems quite undimmed by the passing of the years. But what is it that they would have *me* say?

MILL: 'The refusal of the institutional forms of the bourgeois state finds its expression in the dictatorship of the proletariat.'

MARX: Mmmmm.

MILL: Indeed so.

*There follows a long silence.*

MILL (*very cautiously*): Perhaps your greatest error?

MARX (*with much of his old fire*): I am not at all so sure. Do you think that if the working classes really came to power, even by peaceful and parliamentary means, then those who had lost control of society would simply say, as you English do in your incomprehensible game of cricket: 'Well done, chaps, you have scored more runs than us, the game is yours!' Of course they would not!! Does the tragic experience of the Paris Commune itself teach you nothing? And you can be sure that even if there were no overt violence, then international capitalism would subvert the new workers' government. No, we need to protect our victories, few as they are, by violence and dictatorship if need be.

MILL: Ssssh. The angels might hear you.

MARX: Let them hear me.

MILL: And your carbuncles?

MARX: Let them *not* hear me.

MILL (*trying a new tack*): I agree, sadly, that there is no simple or perhaps even single answer to the dilemma that you have just outlined. And I am no more of a pacifist than you are [*looks anxiously over his shoulder, lest a passing angel be listening*] . . . But if you had spent more time on politics and less on economics? If you had explained more fully what you meant by the dictatorship of the proletariat? I cannot believe that you meant the dictatorship of the party or that of one man alone.

MARX: I did not. In that sense I am not a Marxist, only Karl Marx [*laughs ruefully*]. But if I am not an orthodox Marxist, you are certainly not an orthodox liberal. Ha ha!!

MILL (*very quietly*): I may be in the wrong place to say this, but may God preserve us from orthodoxy of all sorts . . . May we now return for a moment to the question of democracy, the principal subject of our discussion in London so long ago?

MARX: Certainly, though my first love, as you know, is political economy.

MILL: I have a question which has continued to torment me since 1834.

MARX: That is a very long time to have a problem going round and round in one's head. Let us hear it.

MILL: Is it possible to teach people to be democratic? And if it is, what is the best school? You may remember, from your readings of the Classics, the way in which Plato treats the problem of the teaching of virtue in his Dialogues, both in the *Protagoras* and the *Menon*.[1]

MARX: I do indeed.

MILL: Well, at the beginning of the *Menon*, Socrates is asked to choose from three different ways in which virtue may be acquired: by nature, by instruction or by practice. He does not choose, being Socrates. But, reflecting on this problem and transferring it to the realm of democracy, which we both believe to be virtue in its political guise, I cannot conclude that men are naturally democratic, nor even that women are. The twentieth century, which we have observed from here on high . . .

MARX (*in an undertone*): Speak for yourself.

MILL: . . . has demonstrated this in a conclusive fashion. Is then the second proposition correct? That instruction in democracy is sufficient in itself and necessarily implies an inner assumption of democracy? I think not. Many men have had the knowledge of democracy but have then chosen to act in ways far distant from democracy. Mere knowing is not sufficient. There thus remains only our last proposition – that it is the *practice* of democracy that constitutes the true and only school of public virtue.

MARX: Just so. I have argued as much in my pamphlet on the Paris Commune of 1871. All must be involved, in one way or another, in the public domain. And underneath that domain, determining its structure so to speak, must lie another democracy – the economic one. Only a broad parity of resources can assure real democracy – the level playing field of which you all often speak. [*He pauses before continuing with a mischievous expression in his eyes*]

It is no good, you know, leaving all local government in the hands of the rich and educated, as you propose. Nor, in terms of the institutions of a new democracy, can your suggestions about jury service and workers' cooperatives be considered sufficient. The practice of democracy for each individual must be greater and richer than that . . .

Look now [*taking up his telescope*] . . . I espy the London borough of Harrow. In our time it was nothing but a village surrounded by fields. Harrow meant only one of those expensive schools you English love, which you call public precisely because they are private. A very elite school which Lord Byron attended, fitfully if I remember correctly. The school remains, of course, but the fields have gone. But can you see? There they are, the local population, three hundred of them in a great hall, experimenting with citizen control of the annual local budget. What a turn up for the trousers!

MILL (*quietly*): I think you mean 'for the books'.

MARX (*excitedly*): Whatever. But they must be careful – they must make sure that this is a continuous part of democratic local government, not just a publicity stunt.

MILL (*smiling*): It is not quite your proletarian revolution.

MARX: Nor your government by an enlightened elite.

MILL: *Touché!* And now, my dear Karl, may I take you to see the birds of paradise, which are truly magnificent here?

MARX: If you must. But I would greatly prefer to drink strong coffee and continue our discussion.

THE END

# NOTES

## Prelude

1. J. S. Mill to Henry Samuel Chapman, 28 May, 1849, in Mill, *Collected Works* (hereafter *MCW*), Toronto/London, University of Toronto Press/Routledge and Kegan Paul, vol. 14 (1972), p. 33.
2. J. S. Mill, *Chapters on Socialism* (1879), in *MCW*, vol. 5 (1967), pp. 702–53.
3. David McLellan, *Karl Marx: His Life and Thought*, London, Macmillan, 1973, p. 390. For Mill's last years, Nicholas Capaldi, *John Stuart Mill: A Biography*, Cambridge, Cambridge University Press, 2004, pp. 332–65; Michael St John Packe, *The Life of John Stuart Mill*, London, Secker and Warburg, 1954, pp. 473–503. The most sensitive study of Marx's psychology is that of Jerrold Seigel, *Marx's Fate: The Shape of a Life*, Princeton, Princeton University Press, 1978. Isaiah Berlin's biography is still unsurpassed as a short account: *Karl Marx: His Life and Environment*, London, Oxford University Press, 1963 (1st edn 1939), esp. pp. 220–84 for the last years in London.
4. J. S. Mill, *Autobiography* (1873), in *MCW*, vol. 1 (1981), p. 279. See also C. L. Ten, 'Democracy, socialism and the working classes', in John Skorupski (ed.), *The Cambridge Companion to Mill*, Cambridge, Cambridge University Press, 1998, pp. 372–4, and Capaldi, *John Stuart Mill*, p. 327.
5. David Fernbach, 'Introduction', in Karl Marx, *Political Writings*, vol. 3, *The First International and After*, ed. David Fernbach, Harmondsworth, Penguin, 1974, pp. 9–71; J. Braunthal, *History of the International*, vol. 1, *1864–1914*, London, Nelson, 1966.
6. Paul Lafargue, 'Personal recollections of Karl Marx', in D. Ryazanoff (ed.), *Karl Marx: Man, Thinker and Revolutionist*, London, Martin Lawrence, 1927, p. 187.

7. Francis Wheen, *Karl Marx*, London, Fourth Estate, 1999, pp. 387–8. Engels's answers were rather more frivolous. His idea of happiness was a bottle of Château Margaux 1848 and of misery: 'Having to go to the dentist'; Seigel, *Marx's Fate*, p. 265.

8. Mill, *Autobiography*, pp. 264–5.

9. Karl Marx, 'Manifesto of the Communist Party', in Marx, *Political Writings*, vol. 1, *The Revolutions of 1848*, ed. David Fernbach, Harmondsworth, Penguin, 1973, p. 72.

10. Karl Marx, *Critique of the Gotha Programme*, London, Martin Lawrence, 1933, p. 21.

11. Alan Ryan, *J. S. Mill*, London, Routledge and Kegan Paul, 1974, pp. 181–2. For Mill's environmental concerns, see Donald Winch, 'Thinking green, nineteenth-century style: John Stuart Mill and John Ruskin', in Mark Bevir and Frank Trentmann (eds.), *Markets in Historical Contexts*, Cambridge, Cambridge University Press, 2004, pp. 105–28.

12. J. S. Mill, *Principles of Political Economy* (1852), in *MCW*, vol. 3 (1965), p. 754.

13. Paul Smart, *Mill and Marx: Individual Liberty and the Roads to Freedom*, Manchester, Manchester University Press, 1991, p. 163.

14. Marx, *The First International and After*, p. 399. The interview by R. Landor was published on 18 July 1871 in the New York journal *World*. In his revised chapter 'On the probable futurity of the labouring classes', Mill had taken into account the experience of cooperative associations in France between 1848 and 1851, which had 'scattered widely the seeds of future improvement'; *Principles of Political Economy*, pp. 758–96.

15. J. S. Mill, *Considerations on Representative Government* (1861), in *MCW*, vol. 19 (1977), p. 412.

16. Ibid., pp. 433–4. See also J. H. Burns, 'J. S. Mill and democracy, 1829–61', *Political Studies*, vol. 5 (1957), no. 2, pp. 158–75 and no. 3, pp. 281–94. He concludes (pp. 293–4): 'Democracy in the last resort fails by Mill's standards because it rests on an assumption which ran counter to all that he had believed and preached for thirty years – the assumption that men are equal in the moral and intellectual qualities required by the exercise of power.'

17. Karl Marx, 'On the Jewish Question' (1843), in Marx, *Early Writings*, ed. Lucio Colletti, Harmondsworth, Penguin, 1975, pp. 220–21.

18. Karl Marx, 'The Civil War in France: Address of the General Council', in Marx, *The First International and After*, p. 212.

19. The most famous reference is in his letter of 5 March 1852 to Joseph Weydemeyer; K. Marx and F. Engels, *Collected Works*, vol. 39, London, Lawrence and Wishart, 1983, pp. 62–3. See also K. Marx, *Critique of the Gotha Programme*, p. 44.

20. Mill, *Considerations on Representative Government*, p. 571.

21. J. S. Mill to Thomas Smith, 4 October 1872, in *MCW*, vol. 17 (1972), pp. 1910–12.

22. 'The Hague Congress. Reporter's record of the speech made by K. Marx at the meeting held in Amsterdam on September 8, 1872', in Karl Marx and Friedrich Engels, *Selected Works* (2 vols.), Moscow, Foreign Languages Publishing House, 1962, vol. 2, p. 293.

23. William Wordsworth, 'The Two-Part Prelude', in Wordsworth, *Selected Poetry*, ed. Nicholas Roe, Harmondsworth, Penguin, 1992, p. 120.

## *Part I*

1. As Oskar Anweiler explains in his history of the Soviets, their original name was 'councils of workers' delegates'; see his *The Soviets: The Russian Workers', Peasants' and Soldiers' Councils, 1905–21*, New York, Pantheon Books, 1974.

2. V. I. Lenin, 'The tasks of the proletariat in the present revolution' (7 April 1917), in Lenin, *Collected Works*, vol. 24, Moscow, Progress Publishers, 1974, p. 24.

3. V. I. Lenin, 'The State and Revolution' (1917), in Lenin, *On the Paris Commune*, Moscow, n. p., 1970, p. 47.

4. Neil Harding, *Lenin's Political Thought*, vol. 2, London, Macmillan, 1981, pp. 110–41.

5. For soviets as 'quasi-parliamentary bodies, intensively engaged in educating the masses in the practices of democratic elections, political pluralism and parliamentary procedures', see Israel Getzler, 'Soviets as agents of democratisation', in Edith R. Frankel et al. (eds.), *Revolution in Russia: Reassessments of 1917*, Cambridge, Cambridge University Press, 1992, p. 17.

6. Orlando Figes, *Peasant Russia, Civil War: The Volga Countryside in Revolution (1917–1921)*, Oxford, Oxford University Press, 1989, p. 70.
7. Ibid., p. 76. See also the detailed research on Saratov by Donald J. Raleigh, *Experiencing Russia's Civil War: Politics, Society and Revolutionary Culture in Saratov*, Princeton, Princeton University Press, 2002.
8. Rosa Luxemburg, 'The role of organisation in revolutionary activity' (1904), in Robert Looker (ed.), *Rosa Luxemburg: Selected Political Writings*, London, Cape, 1972, pp. 93–105.
9. Mill, *Chapters on Socialism*, p. 737.
10. Indeed, it had already come under heavy fire during the French revolution, when the constitution of 1791, also dependent upon a pyramidal system, had been abandoned in favour of direct elections to the Convention.
11. Edward H. Carr, *The Bolshevik Revolution, 1917–23*, vol. 1, London, Macmillan, 1950, p. 126.
12. Palmiro Togliatti, *Rapporto al IX° congresso del PCI*, in Togliatti, *Opere*, vol. 6, ed. L. Gruppi, Rome, Editori Riuniti, 1984, pp. 413 and 426.
13. For the transitory Chinese interest in the Paris Commune model, see John Bryan Starr, 'Revolution in retrospect: the Paris Commune through Chinese eyes', *China Quarterly*, no. 49, Jan.–March 1972, pp. 106–25.
14. For a more extended discussion, see Paul Ginsborg, *The Politics of Everyday Life: Making Choices, Changing Lives*, London and New Haven, Yale University Press, 2005.
15. Göran Therborn, 'The rule of capital and the rise of democracy', *New Left Review*, first series, no. 103, May–June 1977, pp. 3–41. I have slightly adapted Therborn's scheme by inserting 'intimidation by organised elements of society', with the events of the Terror Election of March 1933 in Germany very much in mind.
16. Larry Diamond and Mark Plattner, 'Introduction', in Diamond and Plattner, *The Global Divergence of Democracies*, Baltimore, Johns Hopkins University Press, 2001, p. x, table 1.
17. Benjamin Constant, 'The liberty of the ancients compared with that of the moderns' (1819), in Constant, *Political Writings*, ed. Bianca Fontana, Cambridge, Cambridge University Press, 1988, p. 317.
18. Ibid., p. 326.

19. *Social Insurance and Allied Services: Report by Sir William Beveridge*, London, Macmillan, 1942, p. 6.
20. Diamond and Plattner (eds.), *The Global Divergence of Democracies*, p. x, table 1.
21. S. Holmberg, 'Down and down we go: political trust in Sweden', in P. Norris (ed.), *Critical Citizens: Global Support for Democratic Government*, Oxford, Oxford University Press, 1999, pp. 103–22, p. 107, figure 5.1.
22. Peter Mair, 'Ruling the void? The hollowing of Western democracy', *New Left Review*, second series, no. 42, Nov.–Dec. 2006, pp. 25–51.
23. Mill, *Considerations on Representative Government*, p. 422. The italics are mine.
24. Robert Michels, *Political Parties: A Sociological Study of the Oligarchical Tendencies of Modern Democracy*, New York, The Free Press, 1962 [1915].
25. John Dunn, *Setting the People Free: The Story of Democracy*, London, Atlantic Books, 2005, p. 50.
26. See, among many others, J. Rifkin, *The European Dream: How Europe's Vision of the Future is Quietly Eclipsing the American Dream*, Cambridge, Polity Press, 2004; M. Leonard, *Why Europe Will Run the 21st Century*, London, Fourth Estate, 2005; G. Morgan, *The Idea of a European Super State*, Princeton/Oxford, Princeton University Press, 2005.
27. S. Fella, 'A Europe of the peoples? New Labour and democratizing the EU', in C. Hoskyns and M. Newman (eds.), *Democratizing the European Union: Issues for the Twenty-first Century*, Manchester, Manchester University Press, 2000, p. 82.
28. Perry Anderson, 'European hypocrisies', *London Review of Books*, vol. 29 (2007), no. 18, p. 17.
29. Peter Mair, 'Popular democracy and the European Union Polity', European Governance Papers (EUROGOV), no. C-05-03 (2005), http://www.connex-network.org/eurogov/pdf/egp-connex-C-05-03.pdf.
30. Anne Muxel, 'Les abstentionnistes', in Pascal Perrineau (ed.), *Le Vote européen, 2004–2005: de l'élargissement au référendum français*, Paris, Presses de la Fondation Nationale des Sciences Politiques, 2005, p. 51, table 1, and p. 55, table 2.

31. A. Rinella, 'Il principio di sussidarietà: definizioni, comparazioni e modello d'analisi', in Rinella et al. (eds.), *Sussidarietà e ordinamenti costituzionali*, Padua, Cedam, 1999.
32. Antonio Estella, *The EU Principle of Subsidiarity and its Critique*, Oxford, Oxford University Press, 2002, p. 177. And he continues (p. 178) even more damningly: 'The Court does not wish to risk its own legitimacy by implementing a principle that is not clearly legal.'
33. Larry Siedentop, *Democracy in Europe*, London, Allen Lane, 2000.
34. Anderson, 'European hypocrisies', p. 18.
35. Tommaso Padoa-Schioppa, *Europa, una pazienza attiva: malinconia e riscatto del Vecchio Continente*, Milan, Rizzoli, 2006, p. 26.

## Part II

1. Naomi Hertz, *The Silent Takeover*, London, Arrow, 2002, p. 8.
2. C. Edwin Baker, *Media Concentration and Democracy: Why Ownership Matters*, Cambridge, Cambridge University Press, 2007.
3. Mill, *Considerations on Representative Government*, p. 404.
4. Ibid., p. 412.
5. J. S. Mill, *On Liberty* (1859), in *MCW*, vol. 5 (1967), p. 212.
6. Ibid., p. 275.
7. Alex Zakaras, 'John Stuart Mill, individuality and participatory democracy', in Nadia Urbinati and Alex Zakaras (eds.), *John Stuart Mill's Political Thought: A Bicentennial Reassessment*, Cambridge, Cambridge University Press, 2007, pp. 217–18.
8. J. S. Mill, *The Subjection of Women* (1869), in *MCW*, vol. 21 (1984), p. 294.
9. Ibid.
10. Ibid., p. 295.
11. See for example his very explicit letter to P. V. Annenkov of 28 December 1846: 'If you assume given stages of development in production, commerce or consumption, you will have a corresponding form of social constitution, a corresponding organisation, whether of the family, of the estates or of the classes – in a word, a correspond-

ing civil society'; Karl Marx and Friedrich Engels, *Collected Works*, vol. 38, London, Lawrence and Wishart, 1982, p. 96.

12. For a more developed discussion of modern families, see Ginsborg, *The Politics of Everyday Life*, pp. 91–128.

13. Stephen Hopgood, *Keepers of the Flame: Understanding Amnesty International*, Ithaca and London, Cornell University Press, 2006. See also V. Finn Heinrich (ed.), *Civicus Global Survey of the State of Civil Society*, Bloomfield CT, Kumarian Press, 2007.

14. J. Kocka, 'Civil society from a historical perspective', *European Review*, vol. 12 (2004), no. 1, pp. 65–79.

15. J. S. Mill, 'De Tocqueville on Democracy in America [II]' (1840), in *MCW*, vol. 18 (1977), p. 165.

16. Nadia Urbinati, *Mill on Democracy: From the Athenian Polis to Representative Government*, Chicago, University of Chicago Press, 2002, p. 67.

17. Mill, *Considerations on Representative Government*, p. 432. See also the valuable comments of Jean Terrier and Peter Wagner, 'Declining deliberation: civil society, community, organised modernity', in Wagner (ed.), *The Languages of Civil Society*, New York, Berghahn, 2006, pp. 83f.

18. Karl Marx, *Capital: A Critical Analysis of Capitalist Production*, vol. 1 [1867; 1st English edn 1887], Moscow, Progress Publishers, 1974, p. 715.

19. Antonio Gramsci, *Selections from the Prison Notebooks*, ed. Quentin Hoare and Geoffrey Nowell Smith, London, Lawrence and Wishart, 1971, p. 238.

20. Norberto Bobbio, *The Future of Democracy: A Defence of the Rules of the Game*, Cambridge, Polity Press, 1987, p. 55. The book comprises a selection of essays written during the 1970s and early 1980s.

21. The Power Inquiry, *Power to the People*, York, York Publishing Distribution, 2006, p. 233.

22. Jon Elster (ed.), *Deliberative Democracy*, Cambridge, Cambridge University Press, 1998, p. 8.

23. Luigi Bobbio, 'Come smaltire i rifiuti: un esperimento di democrazia deliberativa', *Stato e Mercato*, no. 64 (2002), pp. 101–41.

24. Mill, *Considerations on Representative Government*, p. 424.

25. See the discussion in Urbinati, *Mill on Democracy*, pp. 60–65.

26. Marx, 'The Civil War in France', p. 251.

27. Marx, 'On the Jewish Question', p. 234.
28. Mill, *Considerations on Representative Government*, p. 535.
29. Ibid., p. 536.
30. Ibid.
31. A useful recent compendium is John Gastil and Peter Levine (eds.), *The Deliberative Democracy Handbook: Strategies for Effective Civic Engagement in the 21st Century*, San Francisco, Jossey-Bass, 2005.
32. Ibid., pp. 111–19.
33. Ibid., pp. 154–63.
34. Ibid., p. 115.
35. The literature on the Orçamento Participativo is by now extensive. I have found particularly useful M. Gret and Yves Sintomer, *Porto Alegre: l'espoir d'une autre démocratie*, Paris, La Découverte, 2002; Giovanni Allegretti, *L'insegnamento di Porto Alegre: autoprogettualità come paradigma urbano*, Florence, Alinea, 2003; Hilary Wainwright, *Reclaim the State: Experiments in Popular Democracy*, London, Verso, 2003, pp. 42–69.
36. Allegretti, *L'insegnamento di Porto Alegre*, pp. 113–43.
37. S. Baierle, 'The Porto Alegre Thermidor? Brazil's "participatory budget" at the crossroads', *Socialist Register*, 2003, pp. 306 and 307, table 1.
38. A. Fung, 'Deliberative democracy, Chicago style: grass-roots governance in policing and public education', in A. Fung and E. Olin Wright, *Deepening Democracy*, London, Verso, 2003, pp. 111–43.
39. D. Chavez, 'Participation lite: the watering down of people power in Porto Alegre', *Red Pepper*, May 2006; available online at http://www.tni.org/archives/chavez/participation.htm.
40. See his informative recent book: Gianpaolo Baiocchi, *Militants and Citizens: The Politics of Participatory Democracy in Porto Alegre*, Stanford, Stanford University Press, 2005.
41. Power Inquiry, *Power to the People*, pp. 226f.
42. Baiocchi, *Militants and Citizens*, passim. See also his 'The citizens of Porto Alegre', *Boston Review*, March–April 2006. Analytically useful in this context is M.-H. Bacqué, H. Rey and Y. Sintomer, 'Conclusion: La Démocratie participative, modèles et enjeux', in Bacqué, Rey and Sintomer (eds.), *Gestion de proximité et démocratie participative*, Paris, La Découverte, 2006, pp. 293–307, esp. the table 'Cinq modèles participatifs', pp. 298–99.

43. It is worth underlining that this is a very European periodisation, which sees the 1970s as a highpoint of popular participation and the 1980s as a period of retreat and withdrawal. In Brazil, on the contrary, the 1980s witnessed a great explosion of new democratic forms as the country emerged from military dictatorship.

## Part III

1. For further discussion of this point, and the watershed case of *Buckley* v. *Valeo*, heard in the United States Supreme Court in 1976, see Ginsborg, *The Politics of Everyday Life*, pp. 178ff.
2. Robert A. Dahl, *A Preface to Economic Democracy*, Cambridge, Polity Press, 1985, p. 111.
3. Ibid., p. 98.
4. Ibid., p. 73.
5. Marx, 'The Civil War in France', p. 212.
6. Karl Marx, 'Economic and Philosophical Manuscripts', in Marx, *Early Texts*, ed. David McLellan, Oxford, Blackwell, 1972, p. 138.
7. Ibid.
8. Ibid., pp. 136–7, 140.
9. Ibid., pp. 151–2.
10. Ibid., p. 148.
11. Mill, *Chapters on Socialism*, p. 710.
12. Ibid., p. 711.
13. Karl Marx, 'A contribution to the critique of Hegel's *Philosophy of Right*: Introduction', in Marx, *Early Writings*, p. 256.
14. Mill, *Chapters on Socialism*, p. 753.
15. Colin Crouch, *Postdemocracy*, London, Polity Press, 2004, p. 78.
16. Peter Hennessy, *Never Again: Britain 1945–51*, London, Vintage, 1992, p. 174.
17. For the British experience, see the valuable collection of Ken Coates and Anthony Topham (eds.), *Industrial Democracy in Great Britain: A Book of Readings and Witnesses for Workers' Control*, London, MacGibbon and Kee, 1968.
18. Renato Lattes, 'Testimonianza e ricordi: delegati, consigli, sindacato a Torino tra gli anni '60 e '70', in Associazione Biondi-Bartolini and

Fondazione Giuseppe Di Vittorio (eds.), *I due bienni rossi del Novecento, 1919–20 e 1968–69*, Rome, Ediesse, 2006, p. 136.

19. Rudolf Meidner, *Employee Investment Funds: An Approach to Collective Capital Formation*, London, Allen and Unwin, 1978.

20. *Partecipazione e democrazia industriale: ricerca del comitato centrale giovani imprenditori dell' industria*, Milan, Etas, 1977, p. 24.

21. Giulia Barbucci (ed.), *Europa e democrazia industriale: il coinvolgimento dei lavoratori nell'impresa europea*, Rome, Ediesse, 2004.

22. Walter Cerfeda, 'Il coinvolgimento dei lavoratori nella Società Europea', ibid., pp. 13–18.

23. Fernando Vasquez, 'Presente e futuro della Società Europea e della Società Cooperativa Europea', ibid., p. 19.

24. The same observation applies to an earlier comparative work by Graeme Duncan, *Marx and Mill: Two Views of Social Conflict and Social Harmony*, Cambridge, Cambridge University Press, 1973. Neither of them concentrates his attention on the question of democracy.

25. Mill, *The Subjection of Women*, p. 261.

26. The reform of French and Italian family law, which abolished obligatory male headship of households, belongs to the 1970s. India and Bangladesh, on the other hand, are still very far from this objective.

27. Mill, *The Subjection of Women*, p. 276.

28. Ibid., p. 327.

29. Ibid., p. 261.

30. Susan Moller Okin, 'John Stuart Mill's feminism: *The Subjection of Women* and the improvement of mankind', in Maria H. Morales (ed.), *Mill's The Subjection of Women*, Lanham, Rowman and Littlefield, 2005, pp. 24–51.

31. Quoted in Packe, *Mill*, p. 348.

32. Mill, *The Subjection of Women*, p. 298.

33. Marx, 'Manifesto of the Communist Party', p. 84.

34. United Nations Development Programme (UNDP), *Human Development Report No. 6*, Oxford, Oxford University Press, 1995, pp. 29–30.

35. Paul S. Kim, *Japan's Civil Service System: Its Structure, Personnel and Politics*, New York, Greenwood Press, 1988, p. 40.

36. UNDP, *Human Development Report No. 6*, pp. 72–98, esp. tables 3.1 and 3.5.

37. Ibid., p. 52, table 2.8.
38. UNDP, *Human Development Report no. 13*, Oxford, Oxford University Press, 2002, p. 70.
39. Laura Balbo, 'Pensando al prossimo appuntamento: i cento anni del voto alle donne', in Franca Bimbi and Alisa Del Re (eds.), *Genere e democrazia*, Turin, Rosenberg and Sellier, 1997, p. 101.
40. Ibid.
41. For a detailed multi-disciplinary discussion see Bianca Beccalli (ed.), *Donne in quota*, Milan, Feltrinelli, 1999.
42. Franca Bimbi and Alisa Del Re, 'A cinquant'anni dal voto', in Bimbi and Del Re (eds.), *Genere e democrazia*, p. 11.
43. Quoted in Françoise Héritier, *Maschile e femminile: il pensiero della differenza*, Laterza, Roma-Bari, 1997, pp. 195–6.
44. 'Democracy: The ten big questions', *Observer*, 30 Sept. 2007.
45. Martha Nussbaum, *Women and Human Development: The Capabilities Approach*, Cambridge, Cambridge University Press, 2000, p. 242.
46. Mill, *The Subjection of Women*, p. 130.
47. John Downey, 'Participation and/or deliberation', in Lincoln Dahlberg and Eugenia Siapera (eds.), *Radical Democracy and the Internet: Interrogating Theory and Practice*, London, Palgrave Macmillan, 2007, p. 113; *The Times*, 2 Sept. 2006.
48. Downey, 'Participation', pp. 114–15.
49. See, for example, Robert Putnam and Lewis Feldstein, *Better Together: Restoring the American Community*, New York, Simon and Schuster, 2003, p. 9.
50. P. Ferdinand (ed.), *The Internet, Democracy and Democratisation*, London, Frank Cass, 2000; Darin Barney, 'Radical citizenship in the Republic of Technology: a sketch', in Dahlberg and Siapera (eds.), *Radical Democracy and the Internet*, pp. 37–54.
51. In M. Crozier, Samuel P. Huntington and J. Watanuki, *The Crisis of Democracy*, New York, New York University Press, 1975, pp. 12ff.
52. For a sceptical approach, see Robert A. Dahl, 'Can international organizations be democratic? A skeptic's view', in Ian Shapiro and Casiano Hacker Cordón (eds.), *Democracy's Edges*, Cambridge, Cambridge University Press, 1999, pp. 19–36. For a more optimistic view, David Held, 'The transformation of political community: rethinking democracy in the context of globalisation', ibid., pp. 84–111. See also

David Held and Mathias Koenig-Archibugi (eds.), *Global Governance and Public Accountability*, Oxford, Blackwell, 2005.

53. Bruce Ackerman and James Fishkin, *Deliberation Day*, London and New Haven, Yale University Press, 2004.

54. This overall experience has been analysed with considerable insight by Hilary Wainwright in her 'Civil society, democracy and power: global connections', in Helmut Anheier et al. (eds.), *Global Civil Society, 2004–5*, London, Sage, 2005, pp. 95–119.

55. Patrizia Nanz and Jens Steffek, 'Global governance, participation and the public sphere', in Held and Koenig-Archibugi (eds.), *Global Governance*, p. 201.

56. 'Ongoing process for the identification of possible NGO speakers at the HRC High Level Segment'; http://www.ngocongo.org/index. php?what=pag&id=10294.

57. The text of the treaty is available online at http://www.fco.gov.uk/ Files/kfile/CM6429_Treaty.pdf.

58. Ibid.

59. Not all the Union's actions have been so enlightened. It has performed, for instance, a rather less than noble role as the defender of northern European agrarian interests, both within the Union and outside it.

60. Michael Newman, 'Allegiance, legitimation, democracy and the European Union', EUI Working Paper no. 2001/5, San Domenico di Fiesole, EUI, 2001.

61. Although starting from a different viewpoint, the various technical suggestions put forward by Philippe Schmitter in *How to Democratise the European Union . . . and Why Bother?* (Lanham, Rowman and Littlefield, 2000) are of considerable interest.

## Epilogue

1. I am grateful to Gustavo Zagrebelsky for the discussion that follows. See his *Imparare democrazia*, Turin, Einaudi, 2007, esp. pp. 39–47. See also Urbinati, *Mill on Democracy*, pp. 49–54. In the early 1830s Mill translated Plato's Dialogues from the Greek and published them in the *Monthly Repository*.

# BIBLIOGRAPHY

Ackerman, Bruce and Fishkin, James, *Deliberation Day*,
London and New Haven, Yale University Press, 2004

Allegretti, Giovanni, *L'insegnamento di Porto Alegre:
autoprogettualità come paradigma urbano*, Florence,
Alinea, 2003

Anderson, Perry, 'European hypocrisies', *London Review of
Books*, vol. 29 (2007), no. 18, p. 13–21

Anweiler, Oskar, *The Soviets: The Russian Workers', Peasants'
and Soldiers' Councils, 1905–21*, New York, Pantheon
Books, 1974

Bacqué, M.-H., Rey, H. and Sintomer, Y. (eds.), *Gestion
de proximité et démocratie participative*, Paris, La
Découverte, 2006

Baierle, S., 'The Porto Alegre Thermidor? Brazil's
"participatory budget" at the crossroads', *Socialist Register*,
2003

Baiocchi, Gianpaolo, 'The citizens of Porto Alegre', *Boston
Review*, March–April 2006

Baiocchi, Gianpaolo, *Militants and Citizens: The Politics
of Participatory Democracy in Porto Alegre*, Stanford,
Stanford University Press, 2005

Baker, C. Edwin, *Media Concentration and Democracy: Why
Ownership Matters*, Cambridge, Cambridge University
Press, 2007

Balbo, Laura, 'Pensando al prossimo appuntamento: i cento
anni del voto alle donne', in Franca Bimbi and Alisa Del

Re (eds.), *Genere e democrazia*, Turin, Rosenberg and Sellier, 1997

Barbucci, Giulia (ed.), *Europa e democrazia industriale: il coinvolgimento dei lavoratori nell'impresa europea*, Rome, Ediesse, 2004

Barney, Darin, 'Radical citizenship in the Republic of Technology: a sketch', in Lincoln Dahlberg and Eugenia Siapera (eds.), *Radical Democracy and the Internet: Interrogating Theory and Practice*, London, Palgrave Macmillan, 2007, pp. 37–54

Beccalli, Bianca (ed.), *Donne in quota*, Milan, Feltrinelli, 1999

Berlin, Isaiah, *Karl Marx: His Life and Environment*, London, Oxford University Press, 1963 (1st edn 1939)

Bimbi, Franca and Del Re, Alisa (eds.), *Genere e democrazia*, Turin, Rosenberg and Sellier, 1997

Bobbio, Luigi, 'Come smaltire i rifiuti: un esperimento di democrazia deliberativa', *Stato e Mercato*, no. 64 (2002), pp. 101–41

Bobbio, Norberto, *The Future of Democracy: A Defence of the Rules of the Game*, Cambridge, Polity Press, 1987

Braunthal, J., *History of the International*, vol. 1, *1864–1914*, London, Nelson, 1966

Burns, J. H., 'J. S. Mill and democracy, 1829–61', *Political Studies*, vol. 5 (1957), no. 2, pp. 158–75 and no. 3, pp. 281–94

Capaldi, Nicholas, *John Stuart Mill: A Biography*, Cambridge, Cambridge University Press, 2004

Carr, Edward H., *The Bolshevik Revolution, 1917–23*, vol. 1, London, Macmillan, 1950

Cerfeda, Walter, 'Il coinvolgimento dei lavoratori nella Società Europea', in Giulia Barbucci (ed.), *Europa e democrazia industriale: il coinvolgimento dei lavoratori nell'impresa europea*, Rome, Ediesse, 2004, pp. 13–18

Chavez, D., 'Participation lite: the watering down of people power in Porto Alegre', *Red Pepper*, May 2006; available online at http://www.tni.org/archives/chavez/participation.htm

Coates, Ken and Topham, Anthony (eds.), *Industrial Democracy in Great Britain: A Book of Readings and Witnesses for Workers' Control*, London, MacGibbon and Kee, 1968

Constant, Benjamin, *Political Writings*, ed. Bianca Fontana, Cambridge, Cambridge University Press, 1988

Crouch, Colin, *Postdemocracy*, London, Polity Press, 2004

Crozier, M., Huntington, Samuel P. and Watanuki, J., *The Crisis of Democracy*, New York, New York University Press, 1975

Dahl, Robert A., 'Can international organizations be democratic? A skeptic's view', in Ian Shapiro and Casiano Hacker Cordón (eds.), *Democracy's Edges*, Cambridge, Cambridge University Press, 1999, pp. 19–36

Dahl, Robert A., *A Preface to Economic Democracy*, Cambridge, Polity Press, 1985

Diamond, Larry, and Plattner, Mark, *The Global Divergence of Democracies*, Baltimore, Johns Hopkins University Press, 2001

Downey, John, 'Participation and/or deliberation', in Lincoln Dahlberg and Eugenia Siapera (eds.), *Radical Democracy and the Internet: Interrogating Theory and Practice*, London, Palgrave Macmillan, 2007, pp. 108–27

Duncan, Graeme, *Marx and Mill: Two Views of Social Conflict and Social Harmony*, Cambridge, Cambridge University Press, 1973

Dunn, John, *Setting the People Free: The Story of Democracy*, London, Atlantic Books, 2005

Elster, Jon (ed.), *Deliberative Democracy*, Cambridge, Cambridge University Press, 1998

Estella, Antonio, *The EU Principle of Subsidiarity and its Critique*, Oxford, Oxford University Press, 2002

Fella, S., 'A Europe of the peoples? New Labour and democratizing the EU', in C. Hoskyns and M. Newman (eds.), *Democratizing the European Union: Issues for the Twenty-first Century*, Manchester, Manchester University Press, 2000

Ferdinand, P. (ed.), *The Internet, Democracy and Democratisation*, London, Frank Cass, 2000

Figes, Orlando, *Peasant Russia, Civil War: The Volga Countryside in Revolution (1917–1921)*, Oxford, Oxford University Press, 1989

Finn, Heinrich, V. (ed.), *Civicus Global Survey of the State of Civil Society*, Bloomfield CT, Kumarian Press, 2007.

Fung, A., 'Deliberative democracy, Chicago style: grass-roots governance in policing and public education', in A. Fung and E. Olin Wright, *Deepening Democracy*, London, Verso, 2003, pp. 111–43

Gastil, John and Levine, Peter (eds.), *The Deliberative Democracy Handbook: Strategies for Effective Civic Engagement in the 21st Century*, San Francisco, Jossey-Bass, 2005

Getzler, Israel, 'Soviets as agents of democratisation', in Edith R. Frankel et al. (eds.), *Revolution in Russia: Reassessments of 1917*, Cambridge, Cambridge University Press, 1992

Ginsborg, Paul, *The Politics of Everyday Life: Making Choices, Changing Lives*, London and New Haven, Yale University Press, 2005

Gramsci, Antonio, *Selections from the Prison Notebooks*, ed. Quentin Hoare and Geoffrey Nowell Smith, London, Lawrence and Wishart, 1971

Gret M., and Sintomer, Yves, *Porto Alegre: l'espoir d'une autre démocratie*, Paris, La Découverte, 2002

Harding, Neil, *Lenin's Political Thought*, vol. 2, London, Macmillan, 1981

Held, David, 'The transformation of political community: rethinking democracy in the context of globalisation', in Ian Shapiro and Casiano Hacker Cordón (eds.), *Democracy's Edges*, Cambridge, Cambridge University Press, 1999, pp. 84–111

Held, David and Koenig-Archibugi, Mathias (eds.), *Global Governance and Public Accountability*, Oxford, Blackwell, 2005

Hennessy, Peter, *Never Again: Britain 1945–51*, London, Vintage, 1992

Héritier, Françoise, *Maschile e femminile: il pensiero della differenza*, Laterza, Roma-Bari, 1997

Hertz, Naomi, *The Silent Takeover*, London, Arrow, 2002

Holmberg, S., 'Down and down we go: political trust in Sweden', in P. Norris (ed.), *Critical Citizens: Global Support for Democratic Government*, Oxford, Oxford University Press, 1999, pp. 103–22

Hopgood, Stephen, *Keepers of the Flame: Understanding Amnesty International*, Ithaca and London, Cornell University Press, 2006

John Keane, *Democracy and Civil Society*, London, Verso, 1988.

John Keane (ed.), *Civil Society: Berlin Perspectives*, Oxford, Berghahn, 2006.

Kim, Paul S., *Japan's Civil Service System: Its Structure,
Personnel and Politics*, New York, Greenwood Press, 1988

Kocka, J., 'Civil society from a historical perspective',
*European Review*, vol. 12 (2004), no. 1, pp. 65–79

Lafargue, Paul, 'Personal recollections of Karl Marx',
in D. Ryazanoff (ed.), *Karl Marx: Man, Thinker
and Revolutionist*, London, Martin Lawrence, 1927,
pp. 179–208

Lattes, Renato, 'Testimonianza e ricordi: delegati, consigli,
sindacato a Torino tra gli anni '60 e '70', in Associazione
Biondi-Bartolini and Fondazione Giuseppe Di Vittorio
(eds.), *I due bienni rossi del Novecento, 1919–20 e 1968–69*,
Rome, Ediesse, 2006, pp. 129–46

Lenin, V. I., *Collected Works*, vol. 24, Moscow, Progress
Publishers, 1974

Lenin, V. I., 'The State and Revolution' (1917), in Lenin, *On
the Paris Commune*, Moscow, Progress Publishers, n. p.,
1970

Leonard, M., *Why Europe Will Run the 21st Century*, London,
Fourth Estate, 2005

Looker, Robert (ed.), *Rosa Luxemburg: Selected Political
Writings*, London, Cape, 1972

Mair, Peter, 'Popular democracy and the European Union
Polity', European Governance Papers (EUROGOV),
no. C-05–03 (2005), http://www.connex-network.org/
eurogov/pdf/egp-connex-C-05-03.pdf

Mair, Peter, 'Ruling the void? The hollowing of Western
democracy', *New Left Review*, second series, no. 42, Nov.–
Dec. 2006, pp. 25–51

Marx, Karl, *Capital: A Critical Analysis of Capitalist
Production*, vol. 1 [1867; 1st English edn 1887], Moscow,
Progress Publishers, 1974

Marx, Karl, *Critique of the Gotha Programme*, London, Martin Lawrence, 1933

Marx, Karl, *Early Texts*, ed. David McLellan, Oxford, Blackwell, 1972

Marx, Karl, 'On the Jewish Question' (1843), in Marx, *Early Writings*, ed. Lucio Colletti, Harmondsworth, Penguin, 1975, pp. 211–42

Marx, Karl, *Political Writings*, ed. David Fernbach, vol. 1, *The Revolutions of 1848*, Harmondsworth, Penguin, 1973; vol. 2, *Surveys from Exile*, Harmondsworth, Penguin, 1974; vol. 3, *The First International and After*, Harmondsworth, Penguin, 1974

Marx, Karl and Engels, Friedrich, *Collected Works*, vol. 38, London, Lawrence and Wishart, 1982; vol. 39, London, Lawrence and Wishart, 1983

Marx, Karl and Engels, Friedrich, *Selected Works*, 2 vols., Moscow, Foreign Languages Publishing House, 1962

McLellan, David, *Karl Marx: His Life and Thought*, London, Macmillan, 1973

Meidner, Rudolf, *Employee Investment Funds: An Approach to Collective Capital Formation*, London, Allen and Unwin, 1978

Michels, Robert, *Political Parties: A Sociological Study of the Oligarchical Tendencies of Modern Democracy*, New York, The Free Press, 1962 [1915]

Mill, J. S., *Collected Works*, 33 vols., Toronto/London, University of Toronto Press/Routledge and Kegan Paul, 1963–91

Mill, J. S., *On Liberty; with The Subjection of Women and Chapters on Socialism*, ed. Stefan Collini, Cambridge, Cambridge University Press, 1989

Morgan, G., *The Idea of a European Super State*, Princeton/ Oxford, Princeton University Press, 2005

Muxel, Anne, 'Les abstentionnistes', in Pascal Perrineau (ed.), *Le Vote européen, 2004–2005: de l'élargissement au référendum français*, Paris, Presses de la Fondation Nationale des Sciences Politiques, 2005

Nanz, Patrizia and Steffek, Jens, 'Global governance, participation and the public sphere', in David Held and Mathias Koenig-Archibugi (eds.), *Global Governance and Public Accountability*, Oxford, Blackwell, 2005

Newman, Michael, 'Allegiance, legitimation, democracy and the European Union', EUI Working Paper no. 2001/5, San Domenico di Fiesole, EUI, 2001

Nussbaum, Martha, *Women and Human Development: The Capabilities Approach*, Cambridge, Cambridge University Press, 2000

Okin, Susan Moller, 'John Stuart Mill's feminism: *The Subjection of Women* and the improvement of mankind', in Maria H. Morales (ed.), *Mill's 'The Subjection of Women'*, Lanham, Rowman and Littlefield, 2005, pp. 24–51

Padoa-Schioppa, Tommaso, *Europa, una pazienza attiva: malinconia e riscatto del Vecchio Continente*, Milan, Rizzoli, 2006

*Partecipazione e democrazia industriale: ricerca del comitato centrale giovani imprenditori dell' industria*, Milan, Etas, 1977

The Power Inquiry, *Power to the People*, York, York Publishing Distribution, 2006

Putnam, Robert and Feldstein, Lewis, *Better Together: Restoring the American Community*, New York, Simon and Schuster, 2003

Raleigh, Donald J., *Experiencing Russia's Civil War: Politics, Society and Revolutionary Culture in Saratov*, Princeton, Princeton University Press, 2002

Rifkin, J., *The European Dream: How Europe's Vision of the Future is Quietly Eclipsing the American Dream*, Cambridge, Polity Press, 2004

Rinella, A., 'Il principio di sussidarietà: definizioni, comparazioni e modello d'analisi', in A. Rinella et al. (eds.), *Sussidarietà e ordinamenti costituzionali*, Padua, Cedam, 1999

Ryan, Alan, *J. S. Mill*, London, Routledge and Kegan Paul, 1974

Schmitter, Philippe, *How to Democratise the European Union . . . and Why Bother?*, Lanham, Rowman and Littlefield, 2000

Seigel, Jerrold, *Marx's Fate: The Shape of a Life*, Princeton, Princeton University Press, 1978

Siedentop, Larry, *Democracy in Europe*, London, Allen Lane, 2000

Smart, Paul, *Mill and Marx: Individual Liberty and the Roads to Freedom*, Manchester, Manchester University Press, 1991

*Social Insurance and Allied Services: Report by Sir William Beveridge*, London, Macmillan, 1942

St John Packe, Michael, *The Life of John Stuart Mill*, London, Secker and Warburg, 1954

Starr, John Bryan, 'Revolution in retrospect: the Paris Commune through Chinese eyes', *China Quarterly*, no. 49, Jan.–March 1972, pp. 106–25

Ten, C. L., 'Democracy, socialism and the working classes', in John Skorupski (ed.), *The Cambridge Companion to Mill*, Cambridge, Cambridge University Press, 1998

Terrier, Jean and Wagner, Peter, 'Declining deliberation: civil society, community, organised modernity', in Peter Wagner (ed.), *The Languages of Civil Society*, New York, Berghahn, 2006

Therborn, Göran, 'The rule of capital and the rise of democracy', *New Left Review*, first series, no. 103, May–June 1977, pp. 3–41

Togliatti, Palmiro, *Rapporto al IX° congresso del PCI*, in Palmiro Togliatti, *Opere*, vol. 6, ed. L. Gruppi, Rome, Editori Riuniti, 1984

United Nations Development Programme, *Human Development Report No. 6*, Oxford, Oxford University Press, 1995

United Nations Development Programme, *Human Development Report no. 13*, Oxford, Oxford University Press, 2002

Urbinati, Nadia, *Mill on Democracy: From the Athenian Polis to Representative Government*, Chicago, University of Chicago Press, 2002

Vasquez, Fernando, 'Presente e futuro della Società Europea e della Società Cooperativa Europea', in Giulia Barbucci (ed.), *Europa e democrazia industriale: il coinvolgimento dei lavoratori nell'impresa europea*, Rome, Ediesse, 2004

Wainwright, Hilary, 'Civil society, democracy and power: global connections', in Helmut Anheier et al. (eds.), *Global Civil Society, 2004–5*, London, Sage, 2005, pp. 95–119

Wainwright, Hilary, *Reclaim the State: Experiments in Popular Democracy*, London, Verso, 2003

Wheen, Francis, *Karl Marx*, London, Fourth Estate, 1999

Winch, Donald, 'Thinking green, nineteenth-century style: John Stuart Mill and John Ruskin', in Mark Bevir and

Frank Trentmann (eds.), *Markets in Historical Contexts*, Cambridge, Cambridge University Press, 2004, pp. 105–28

Wordsworth, William, *Selected Poetry*, ed. Nicholas Roe, Harmondsworth, Penguin, 1992

Zagrebelsky, Gustavo, *Imparare democrazia*, Turin, Einaudi, 2007

Zakaras, Alex, 'John Stuart Mill, individuality and participatory democracy', in Nadia Urbinati and Alex Zakaras (eds.), *John Stuart Mill's Political Thought: A Bicentennial Reassessment*, Cambridge, Cambridge University Press, 2007, pp. 200–220

# INDEX

Harrow Open Budget
  Process 73
health services 87
Hitler, Adolf 23
Holland
  European elections
    (2004) 34
  votes against the
    proposed European
    Constitution 34, 114
home living 28, 29, 42
human rights 111–12
Hungary: European
  elections (2004) 34
Huntington, Samuel 106

**I**

income, inequalities of 6
India: women councillors
  97, 98
Indian Civil Service 8
Indian sub-continent:
  growth of civil society
  50–51
individualism/individuality
  44–5, 48, 52, 120
industrial proletariat, Marx
  favours political power
  for 8
information technology
  103–5
INGOS (international

non-governmental
  organisations) 110, 111
insurance services 87
intergovernmentalism 33
International Convention
  against Enforced
  Disappearances 112
International Criminal
  Court 31
International Working
  Men's Association:
  Nottingham Branch 9
internet 104, 105
Iraq war 30
Italian Communist Party,
  Ninth Congress of the
  (1960) 20
Italian factory councils 88
Italy: gender parity issue 97

**J**

Japan: gender parity issue 97
Joseph Rowntree Trust 59
jury service 52

**K**

Kandic, Natasa 12
Kerry, John 28
Kocka, Jürgen 50
Kofi kari-kari ('King
  Coffee') 1
Kyoto Agreement 30–31